A FIRESIDE BOOK
PUBLISHED BY SIMON & SCHUSTER, INC.
NEW YORK

Ceil Dyer

*P*ASTA

AND OTHER

SPECIAL

SALADS

10 9 8 7 6 5

Library of Congress Cataloging in Publication Data

Dyer, Ceil.
    Pasta and other special salads.

    "A Fireside book"
    Includes index.
    1. Salads.   2. Cookery (Macaroni). I. Title.
TX740.D973   1987   641.8'3   86-27027
ISBN: 0-671-50880-6

Contents

Introduction

These days we Americans no longer eat as we once did a few short years ago. We no longer even think about food in the same way. We're much more concerned with the way we look and the way we feel and, of course, we're much more sophisticated, more knowledgeable about food. Gone are the days when mother prepared that same old blue plate special each day: meat, potatoes, and vegetable. We no longer have time, nor do we want such filling and fattening fare. Salads are no longer just an afterthought, a wedge of iceberg issue, a slice of tomato drowned in a commercially prepared bottled dressing, something to be eaten only because it is "good for us." And thank goodness for that.

In our new American cuisine, salads have taken on much more importance. They have become the first course, the main course, or the most important part of a buffet supper. Instead of something just tacked onto the menu as an afterthought, a great salad is often the star of the meal.

The difference between a good salad and a positively great-tasting salad is not so much what ingredients you use as how you prepare and combine them. If you are lazy and just dump everything together, the salad will not come out as well as when you add each ingredient one at a time, in its logical sequence. Preparing a great salad is like preparing any other type recipe—short cuts compromise quality.

When preparing a salad relatively new to your culinary repertoire or if you're unfamiliar with the method of preparation, start by reading the recipe all the way through. Note what ingredients should be prepared first and what preparation can be done ahead of time. Next, check to see if you have all the required ingredients and, if not, what ingredients you have on hand can serve as substitutes. Check, too, to see if you have all the necessary equipment for easy preparation as well as the necessary serving dishes, bowls, and so forth.

A salad can be as simple as fresh, crisp lettuce tossed just before serving with oil, vinegar, salt, and pepper, or it can begin with a hearty, flavorful base of pasta, rice, potatoes, or beans combined with crisp vegetables, delectable seafood, or savory meats. Such salads can be put together with a seemingly endless variety of different dressings, and they can be garnished in many different ways.

This book is a collection of the best of such recipes. That they can be made ahead and are easy to prepare are only minor parts of their attraction. Of much more importance is that they taste positively grand. Feel free, however, to change or adapt them to your own taste, as well as that of your family and friends. Or you can use these recipes as a take-off point to prepare your own special creations. After all, that's how all great recipes, all great salads first came into being.

THE GREENING
OF A SALAD

1.

As any good cook will tell you, all fine food requires a goodly amount of tender loving care, and great salads are no exception.

Though no complicated cooking is required for any of the salads in this book, extra time must be given to selecting, storing, and preparing each ingredient or your salad will fall short of your expectations. Lettuce and other greens must be crisp, vegetables unblemished, and fruits at their peak of perfection. And because a dressing is all important to any salad, it's essential to seek out the very best place to buy fine imported olive oils as well as flavorful vinegars, assorted olives, capers, anchovies, and the many other elegant additions that can elevate your salad from simple to simply sublime.

So in this short section I've attempted to cover a number of basics that will help make your salad "the best ever." For example, you'll find here how to select and store lettuce; how to prepare vegetables, which ones can be served raw and which are best if blanched or crisp cooked; how to select and prepare tomatoes so that they give up their best flavor; and even a mini-course on olive oils, vinegars, and such.

I hope these few pages will contribute in some measure to what is, after all, the easiest yet best of all food preparation—the making of a great salad.

LETTUCE

Because lettuce and other greens are so varied in taste, texture, and color, they can make a dramatic difference in flavor when combined with other salad ingredients.

ARUGULA: Deep green leaves and pungent flavor. Combine with other greens when adding to salad or use as a colorful garnish.

BELGIAN ENDIVE: A small, elongated lettuce with a tight head; crisp in texture with an elegant and very distinctive flavor. Use whole leaves to garnish salad bowls or individual salad plates. Chop or cut into thin slices to add to salads. Do not prepare until ready to use or leaves will darken.

BIBB LETTUCE: Small, tight heads with fragile leaves and a faintly sweet taste.

BOSTON LETTUCE: Loosely packed small heads of pale green leaves. Hearty yet pleasant flavor.

CHICORY: Tart, crisp leaves. Use in small quantities with other, less aggressive lettuce or with vegetables.

ICEBERG LETTUCE: Least flavorful and nutritious of all salad greens. Crisp, large, green outer leaves make a pleasant lining for a salad bowl or individual plates. When cut across into thin shreds, it adds crunchy texture.

LEAF LETTUCE: The flavorful, tender leaves from the numerous varieties of leaf lettuce are rather soft in texture, and curly green or red-tipped. They are especially flavorful when young.

PARSLEY: Though these feathery sprigs make a beautiful garnish, they are rarely eaten because they are too aggressive in flavor. When trimmed and minced, however, their aggressiveness is tamed, and they add marvelous flavor to the salad.

RADICCHIO: Miniature bright red leaves with a slightly astringent flavor. They add both character and color when mixed in small quantity with other greens.

RED LEAF LETTUCE: This crinkly leaf lettuce is deep purply-red. It adds color as well as mild and pleasurable flavor when combined with other salad ingredients.

ROMAINE: Long heads of firm, tight leaves with a robust flavor. Best when trimmed, then cut across into narrow shreds.

WATERCRESS: These deep green cloverlike leaves make a beautiful garnish for any salad.

Preparing lettuce for salads

LETTUCE: If lettuce has been wrapped and sealed in plastic wrap, unwrap it as soon as possible (without air it will quickly become dry and wilted).

LOOSE LEAF LETTUCE: Remove and discard tough stem ends. Separate leaves and one at a time rinse under a thin, steady stream of cold water. Stack wet leaves and wrap loosely in double-thick paper toweling. Sprinkle outer wrap with sufficient water to completely moisten. Place wrapped package in the vegetable bin of the refrigerator. Leaves will be crisp and completely dry in 1–2 hours.

FIRM HEADS OF LETTUCE: Remove and discard damaged outer leaves. Tear, do not cut, into bite-size chunks. Place chunks into colander and rinse under cold running water. Shake colander to remove excess water, then transfer chunks to paper toweling and wrap loosely as described above.

You can store wrapped lettuce leaves and chunks in the crisper bin of the refrigerator up to 24 hours. Sprinkle with additional water if outer wrap becomes dry.

Vegetables that should be blanched, steamed, or crisp cooked

Though you will sometimes find fresh broccoli, cauliflower, carrots, green beans, and peas served raw at a restaurant salad bar, their flavor will be vastly improved if they are first blanched, steam blanched, or crisp cooked.

TO BLANCH: Use this method for preparing a large quantity of vegetables. Bring a large pot of water to a full boil and add vegetables. Let water return to a full boil and boil for about 30 seconds. Drain into colander and immediately rinse under cold running water. Blot thoroughly dry before adding to salads.

TO STEAM: Bring 1 inch of water to a boil in a large steamer pot or saucepan. Place vegetables (cut up or whole) in a metal vegetable steamer and place steamer inside pot. Cover tightly and steam vegetables until their colors brighten considerably and they are just tender. Drain into colander and rinse under cold water to stop cooking process.

TO CRISP COOK VEGETABLES FOR SALADS: Steam as above but increase cooking time until vegetables have lost their raw taste.

BROCCOLI: Break broccoli flowerets from stems and separate large flowerets into bite-size pieces; trim stems. Cut large stems across into thin slices or cut them into approximately ½-inch-thin strips. Place flowerets and stems in a large bowl and cover with about 2 inches of cold water. Stir in about 1 teaspoon of salt and let stand about 5 minutes, stirring occasionally. Dirt and sand will sink to the bottom of the bowl; foreign matter will float to the top. Pour off top water, then lift flowerets and stems from the bowl and transfer to a large colander. Drain and blot dry. Crisp cook as directed.

CAULIFLOWER: Remove and discard leaves and root end; break into bite-size flowerets. Place flowerets into colander and rinse under cold running water. Crisp cook as directed.

CARROTS: Trim carrots and scrape off skin with a small, sharp knife or vegetable scraper. Cut at a 45-degree angle into oval slices or cut across into the thinnest possible slices. For julienne strips, cut carrots into ½-inch pieces, then cut lengthwise into narrow slices; stack and cut lengthwise into julienne strips. You can blanch, steam, or crisp cook as directed.

FRESH GREEN SNAP BEANS: Place beans into colander and rinse under cold running water. Snip off ends. Pour sufficient water into a large, heavy skillet to come to a depth of about 2 inches. Bring to a full boil over high heat. Add beans, cover, and cook 8–10 minutes, only until crisp-tender and no raw taste remains. Transfer to a colander and rinse immediately under cold running water to stop the cooking process.

FRESH GREEN PEAS: Fill a large, heavy skillet or saucepan to a depth of about 2 inches with water. Place over high heat and bring to a boil. Add peas, cover, and cook 1–2 minutes, only until no raw taste remains. Drain into colander and rinse immediately under cold running water to stop the cooking process. Blot dry before adding to salad.

FROZEN GREEN PEAS: Place a frozen block of peas into colander; let stand at room temperature until thawed. Blot thoroughly dry and add to salad without cooking.

PREPARING RAW VEGETABLES

Unwrap and store in the crisper bin of the refrigerator. Prepare just before using.

CUCUMBERS: With the exception of the relatively new, very long, thin, seedless cucumbers that are wrapped and sealed in plastic wrap, most store-bought cucumbers are heavily waxed to keep them fresh and attractive. They should be peeled before using and the seeds removed: Cut the peeled cucumbers in half lengthwise and, using a spoon, simply scoop center seeds and discard. Slice, dice, or chop cucumbers following recipe directions.

GREEN, RED, OR YELLOW BELL PEPPERS: To cut into thin strips, remove and discard rounded ends or save for other use. Cut each pepper into 4 wedges from top to bottom. Remove and discard seeds and white ribs. Cut lengthwise into narrow strips. To cut into rounds, cut off top and bottom end pieces, cut across into thin slices, remove and discard center seeds and white rib, and dice or chop following recipe directions.

MUNG BEAN SPROUTS AND OTHER SPROUTS: Place sprouts in a large bowl and cover with about 2 inches of hot water. Dirt and sand will sink to the bottom; loose hulls will float to the top. Gently pour off top water with hulls. Lift sprouts from water and transfer to paper toweling. Blot dry with additional paper toweling.

ONIONS: Peel and cut across into thin slices and separate slices into rings. To chop, remove and discard peel. Cut in half from top to bottom. Place halves flat side down on cutting board; cut across, first vertically, then horizontally.

GREEN ONIONS (SCALLIONS): Cut off and discard root ends. Cut off and discard all but about 2 inches of green tops. On chopping board, cut into thin slices.

GARLIC: To peel garlic cloves, place one at a time on cutting board. Press down firmly with the flat side of a cleaver until slightly crushed. Pull off and discard peel, then crush the peeled garlic again with the flat side of the knife. To chop, hold the tip of the cleaver on the chopping board and cut the garlic clove horizontally, then vertically into small dice. To mince, push the dice together on the chopping board and chop until so finely minced that pieces will hold together when rolled into a ball.

MUSHROOMS: Cut off and discard tough stem ends. Hold mushrooms one at a time under cold running water. Rub clean with your fingers. Immediately blot dry with paper toweling. (Wet mushrooms left standing will absorb moisture and lose flavor.) Cut them across into thin T shapes or chop, dice, or mince following recipe directions.

CELERY: Remove leafy end pieces and save for other use. Remove and discard tough ends. Peel off tough strings. Place celery on its side on a chopping board. Cut across at a 45-degree angle into thin crescent-shaped slices. To cut into julienne strips, cut trimmed celery stalks across into about ½-inch slices, then cut lengthwise into narrow strips. Chop, dice, or mince following recipe directions.

ZUCCHINI: Trim off and discard end pieces; do not peel. Rinse briefly under cold running water and blot thoroughly dry. With a small, sharp knife scrape off any damaged skins. Cut at a 45-degree angle into very thin oval slices or cut across into ½-inch lengths. Cut lengths across into thin slices; stack slices and cut lengthwise into narrow strips.

FRESH SPINACH: Wash each leaf under cold running water and blot thoroughly dry. Remove and discard tough stems. Tear into small pieces or cut across into narrow shreds.

These greens can be prepared ahead of time:

PARSLEY: Remove and discard tough stems. Rinse under cold running water; shake off excess water, then wrap loosely in double-thick paper toweling. Sprinkle top layer of toweling with sufficient cold water to moisten thoroughly. Store wrapped package in the vegetable storage bin of the refrigerator for up to 24 hours. Moisten outer layer of toweling if it becomes dry. Use parsley sprigs for garnish. To use in salads, place parsley on chopping board and, using a heavy cleaver, chop until so finely minced that pieces hold together when rolled into a ball.

WATERCRESS: Remove and discard tough stems. Use watercress sprigs as garnish or tear leaves into small pieces and add to salad.

SELECTING AND PREPARING TOMATOES

There are a number of different varieties of tomatoes in the market today, but only one type should be used in a salad—vine-ripened. Grow your own, beg or barter them from your neighbor's garden, or buy them from a roadside stand or from a market that features locally grown produce. Don't add tomato slices or wedges to any salad; the juice will water down your dressing and, unless the tomatoes are cut into bite-size pieces, the salad will be difficult to eat with only a fork.

TO PREPARE TOMATOES TO ADD TO SALADS: Rinse tomatoes 1 at a time under cold running water and blot dry. Cut each in half and gently squeeze out juice and all possible seeds. Place halves on cutting board and cut lengthwise into narrow strips. Blot strips thoroughly dry and remove any remaining seeds before adding to salad.

TO PREPARE TOMATO CASES FOR STUFFING: Cut a thick slice from the top of each tomato. With a small knife or sharp-edged spoon, scoop out center pulp, then discard all seeds and juice. Chop pulp and blot thoroughly dry; reserve to add to salad if desired. Sprinkle inside of tomato cases lightly with salt. Place upside down on paper toweling to drain for about 15 minutes or until ready to stuff with salad mixture.

TO PEEL TOMATOES: If preparing only 1 or 2 very large, ripe tomatoes, spear each with a long-handled fork and hold under very hot running water for about 5 seconds. Blot dry, then rub skin with the blunt side of a small knife until it loosens and becomes slightly dark. Pierce the skin with the knife point and pull off the peel.

For a larger quantity of tomatoes, bring a large pot of water to a full boil, then pierce tomatoes one at a time with a long-handled fork and hold in the boiling water for 10–30 seconds. The riper the tomato, the less time it takes. Rinse under cold running water, then peel off the skin with a small, sharp knife. If the skin sticks, return the tomato to hot water until it loosens. If desired, cut each tomato in half, gently squeeze out seeds and juice, cut into small cubes, and add to salads. Or cut tomatoes into thick slices and serve as an accompaniment to salads. See recipe for Sliced Tomatoes Sicilian-Style on page 160.

Fresh herbs

When substituting fresh herbs for dried herbs, use about 2 tablespoons of minced herbs for each ¼–½ teaspoon of dried herbs. To wash, fill a large bowl with cold water. Add the herbs and stir briefly; dirt or sand will sink to the bottom. Lift herbs from water and blot thoroughly dry with paper toweling. Tear leaves from stems and, with your hands, tear into small pieces or place herbs with stems on chopping board. Use a small, sharp knife to chop or mince, following recipe directions.

Olives

"And garnish with olives." How many recipes do you have in your collection that end with this line? In my files there are too many to count. Though olives do add an elegant touch to just about any dish, they can be much more than just a garnish, adding a depth of flavor to even the simplest salad. These are some of my favorite kinds.

ALFONSO: Extra large and juicy with a full, meaty taste.

CALABRESE: A bronze-green olive with a mild yet assertive flavor. Delicious.

KALAMATA: This large, almond-shaped purply-black olive from Greece is perhaps our most popular import.

GREEK BLACK OLIVE: These small, round, brine-cured olives are most frequently found sold in bulk at your favorite delicatessen.

NIÇOISE: Our favorite olive. This small black olive is first cured in brine, then packed in oil. This is the perfect olive for Salade Niçoise (see page 118).

ROYAL AND VICTORIA: Jumbo black olives from California or Greece, cured in fragrant but mild olive oil. Elegant.

CRACKED GREEN OLIVES: These Sicilian beauties are salt-cured, then flavored with oregano and pepper.

PIMIENTO-STUFFED OLIVES: Tangy yet mild, they come in a variety of sizes. When sliced, they add a splash of color to any salad.

OLIVE AND OTHER OILS

Contrary to popular opinion, the best olive oil you can buy is not always the most expensive, it's the freshest. Buy olive oil in a gourmet food shop, an Italian grocery, or one of our new super-supermarkets. If left on a grocer's shelf for more than a short time (2–3 months), it will darken and become rancid in the unopened bottle. Unless you are a chef in an Italian restaurant, buy olive oil in small quantities. Once opened, store this oil in the refrigerator—never at room temperature, under neon lighting, or in direct sunlight. Though it will thicken and look cloudy when cold, it will clear and thin out as soon as it reaches room temperature, in 10–15 minutes.

EXTRA-VIRGIN OLIVE OIL: This oil is made from the very first pressing of the olives. When very fresh it is pale to dark green, depending on the filtering the oil has undergone. Its flavor and aroma are the same as green olives.

VIRGIN OLIVE OIL: This oil is also made exclusively from the oil of the fruit, though it may be from a second pressing. It should have a smooth, faintly sweet and nutty flavor.

PURE OLIVE OIL: This oil is made from extracting the previously pressed olive pulp with added solvents. Okay for cooking or frying, but not good enough for salad making.

ALMOND, HAZELNUT, AND WALNUT OILS: Expensive but well worth the price. Sweet and delicate, and splendid to use for vinaigrette dressings. Since these oils tend to lose flavor and become rancid, buy in small quantities and use soon after opening.

HERB-FLAVORED OILS: Olive or grapeseed oils that have been flavored with herbs or spices. Tarragon is our favorite, but other herbs such as basil, bay leaf, garlic, and peppercorn are also used.

PEPPER OILS: Delicately flavored oils from grapeseed that are spiced with pepper.

OTHER OILS FOR SALAD MAKING: Safflower or peanut oil with a slight, very delicate flavor, or pure, unflavored vegetable oils are best suited for mayonnaise and other thick salad dressings. They can be combined with olive oil for added richness, if desired.

VINEGARS

Though salad dressings use less vinegar than oil, the vinegar is of equal importance. I bypass distilled vinegars that are made from grains such as rye, corn, barley, and malt. I find them too acid for the subtle art of great salad making.

WINE VINEGARS: Made from red or white wine, sherry, and even champagne. They add subtle, delectable flavor.

FRUIT VINEGARS: Light and fresh-tasting, these vinegars are becoming increasingly popular. Raspberry vinegar is our favorite, but you will also find vinegars flavored with many other fruits, including blueberries, blackberries, cherries, and peaches.

HERB VINEGARS: Prepared by adding herbs to wine or cider vinegar. Tarragon vinegar is best known, but other herbs include oregano, thyme, and rosemary. Can now be found in most gourmet food shops.

CIDER VINEGAR: The apples from which it is made give a tart, crisp flavor to this all-purpose classic.

BALSAMIC VINEGAR: This slowly aged vinegar belongs in a class by itself. Its incredible flavor, deep reddish brown color and sweet-sour taste is produced by adding the must of the grape to oak barrels that store the vinegar. As it ages, the vinegar is transferred first to chestnut, then mulberry, and finally juniper wood barrels, and the resulting taste bears traces of flavor from each. Because of the slow aging process, this vinegar is usually much more expensive than any other variety, but it's well worth the price.

PASTA PERFECT SALADS

2.

What goes into a pasta salad? To our way of thinking, that depends very much on when, where, and how you serve it. In Italy, where no meal seems complete without pasta, a small portion of pasta salad is often served as a first course. Here in America we are more apt to serve pasta salads as a main-course dish, and we match them to the seasons and what is available in the market.

For a summertime luncheon we often serve linguine salad with fresh garden vegetables cut into long, thin julienne strips. Or we serve fettuccine with fresh pesto, made from our summertime crop of basil. For large dinner parties served buffet-style, we stay with small pasta shapes that are much easier to eat than long strands, and we add not only a goodly assortment of fresh vegetables but also whatever else the budget allows: fresh shrimp or crab meat, imported canned tuna, baked ham, or thin strips of rare roast beef. In addition, we often include imported olives or capers or, when we can afford it, thin strips of smoked salmon.

Included here is a varied collection of pasta salads ranging from budget fare to creations that "just this once ignore the expense." Each one has been tested, tasted, and found by family and friends to be quite a bit better than good. We hope you will agree.

COOKING PERFECT PASTA

It's so simple; almost everyone knows how to cook pasta. Just read the directions on the package. Is that all? No, not quite, as a good Italian chef will tell you. Though pasta cooking is easy, there are a few tricks of the trade.

For pasta salads especially, the pasta should be cooked only until *al dente*, which literally means "firm to the tooth."

Fill an 8-quart pot with 4–6 quarts of water and bring to a full boil. Stir in 1 teaspoon of salt and 1–2 teaspoons of peanut or vegetable oil. The oil not only keeps the pasta from sticking together, it also prevents the water from boiling over the pot. Add about one-fourth of the pasta at a time so that the water continues to simmer. It will quickly return to a full boil when all the pasta has been added. Stir once with a long-handled wooden fork or spoon, then stir occasionally as the pasta cooks to keep the strands separate. Test by tasting—it's the only way.

Most pastas take less time to cook than the package directions tell you. When the pasta is cooked to your taste, immediately add 2 cups of cold water (this stops the cooking process). Drain at once into large colander, then shake the colander back and forth to drain off any remaining water. While still hot, transfer to a large bowl and immediately add 1–2 tablespoons of olive or vegetable oil, stirring it in with a long-handled wooden fork. Add any other ingredients you have prepared for the salad. Toss and mix thoroughly, then serve at room temperature.

PASTA, PASTA, PASTA

Not so long ago, we Americans didn't eat pasta. Though we have always eaten oodles of noodles as well as miles of spaghetti, we thought of pasta only as something we ordered in an Italian restaurant. But what's in a name? These days pasta is as American as pie—pizza pie, that is, and what could be more American than that? To clear up any remaining confusion, however, here is a list of the Italian pasta shapes we have used in this book followed by a short description.

BUCATINI: short, straight macaroni

CAPELLINI: very, very thin spaghetti

CAPELVENERE: fine noodles

CAVATELLI: small, short, crinkled-edge shells

DITALI: small, short macaroni

FARFALLE: "butterflies"; bowties

FEDELINI: very fine spaghetti

FETTUCCINE: very narrow ribbons

LINGUINE: narrow ribbons

MACARONI: tubular or hollow pasta

MARUZZE: "seashells"

MEZZANI: short, cut, curved macaroni

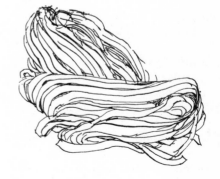

ORZO: rice-shaped pasta

PASTA VERDE: green pasta flavored and colored with spinach

RIGATONI: large, grooved macaroni

ROTELLE: pasta twists

SPAGHETTINI: very thin spaghetti

TORTELLINI: small, square cheese-, meat-, or vegetable-stuffed pasta

VERMICELLI: very fine spaghetti

ZITI: large, slightly curved tubes

You will also find recipes prepared with:

CHINESE NOODLES (MEIN): very fine Oriental noodles that do not require cooking

AMERICAN PASTA SALAD DELI-STYLE

You never had it so good.

8 ounces small pasta shapes, such as cavatelli, rotelle, and farfalle
2 tablespoons mild olive oil, or 1 tablespoon vegetable oil and 1 tablespoon olive oil
1 tablespoon apple cider vinegar
1 teaspoon salt
Coarsely ground black pepper to taste
½ cup chopped imported Genoa salami
½ cup chopped cooked breast of turkey

½ cup chopped baked Virginia ham
½ cup (approximately 2–3 ounces) chopped Swiss cheese
¼ cup chopped black olives
1 small Vidalia or purple onion, chopped
2 stalks celery, minced
1 small green pepper, chopped
¾ cup mayonnaise, preferably homemade (see page 181)
Crisp lettuce leaves
Tomato wedges for garnish

Cook pasta following directions on page 26. Drain and immediately transfer to a large bowl. Add oil, vinegar, salt, and pepper. Toss to mix. Let stand until cooled to room temperature. Add salami, turkey, ham, cheese, olives, onion, celery, and green pepper. Spoon mayonnaise over surface. Toss salad again to thoroughly incorporate ingredients. If desired, refrigerate until ready to serve.

Spoon salad into a lettuce-lined bowl. Garnish, if desired, with tomato wedges.

Makes 6 servings.

Fettuccine fettini

In Italian, the word *fettini* means strip. In this recipe, narrow strips of pasta are combined with equally narrow strips of ham and cheese. Both are dressed with a garlicky vinaigrette.

¼ cup tarragon vinegar
1 teaspoon Dijon mustard
¼ cup peanut or vegetable oil
¼ cup olive oil, or ¼ cup peanut or vegetable oil
1 clove garlic, minced
2 tablespoons minced parsley
8 ounces Emmenthaler or other imported Swiss cheese, cut into julienne strips ¼ inch by 2 inches

8 ounces mortadella or baked Virginia ham, cut into julienne strips ¼ inch by 2 inches
8 ounces fettuccine or other long strands of pasta cut across at 2-inch lengths
Salt to taste
Coarsely ground black pepper to taste

In a large bowl, combine vinegar and mustard. Beat until blended, then slowly add the peanut oil and olive oil, beating as added. Stir in garlic and parsley. Add cheese and ham strips.

Cook fettuccine following directions on page 26. Drain into colander and, while still hot, add to ham and cheese mixture. Toss to mix. Season to taste with salt and pepper. Serve at room temperature. Serve, if desired, with Bloody Mary Carrots (see page 159).

Makes 6 servings.

good

PASTA SALAD WITH CHICKEN AND FRUIT

Grapes and pineapple in combination with freshly cooked chicken give this salad a delicate flavor.

1 8-ounce can pineapple chunks
   Pineapple Mayonnaise (see below)
4 halved chicken breasts, cooked and cut into bite-size pieces
1 stalk celery with leaves, coarsely chopped
½ cup chopped red or green bell pepper

¼ cup sliced scallions or green onions
½ cup slivered almonds
1 cup seedless white grapes
8 ounces rotelle
   Salt and pepper to taste

PINEAPPLE MAYONNAISE
1 cup thick mayonnaise, preferably homemade (see page 181)
2 tablespoons pineapple juice drained from can
1 teaspoon fresh lemon juice
   Salt to taste
   Pepper to taste

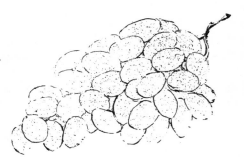

Drain pineapple chunks into colander and reserve juice for dressing. Place paper toweling over pineapple chunks to absorb moisture. Set aside.

Prepare Pineapple Mayonnaise. In a medium bowl, mix all ingredients thoroughly. Set aside.

Place chicken in a large bowl. Stir in chopped celery, red or green pepper, onion, almonds, grapes, and pineapple. Cover and refrigerate until ready to use.

Cook pasta following directions on page 26. Drain into colander, then transfer to a large bowl. Add Pineapple Mayonnaise and chicken mixture. Toss to mix. Add salt and pepper to taste. Transfer to a salad bowl. If desired, refrigerate until about 30 minutes before serving.

Makes 6–8 servings.

CARROT AND ORZO SALAD

This is no more than a slightly sophisticated version of an old favorite, carrot salad, mixed with pasta—but oh, what a difference it makes.

½ cup (approximately 2 ounces) chopped mixed dried fruit
2 tablespoons sherry wine vinegar
1 pound fresh carrots, scraped, trimmed, and coarsely grated
⅓ cup peanut or vegetable oil
1 teaspoon salt
Pepper to taste
1–2 dashes of allspice
8 ounces orzo
¼ cup minced parsley
1 tablespoon finely chopped fresh basil leaves

Place diced fruit and vinegar in the bowl of a food processor; process only until fruit is finely minced. Transfer to a large bowl. Trim and scrape carrots on the coarse side of a hand grater or place in the bowl of a food processor and process until coarsely grated. Add to fruit-vinegar mixture. Add oil, salt, pepper, and allspice. Toss with 2 forks to mix. Cover bowl and refrigerate salad for several hours or overnight. Remove from refrigerator about 30 minutes before using.

Cook orzo following directions on page 26. Drain into colander, then add to carrot mixture. Add parsley and basil. Toss salad to mix thoroughly.

Makes 6–8 servings.

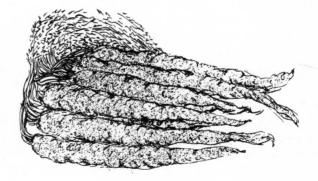

CHICKEN AND SHELLS WITH CURRIED MAYONNAISE

Here is a refreshing hearty salad that can be prepared a day in advance, thus freeing you for other preparations the day of your party.

Curried Mayonnaise Dressing
(see below)
8 ounces small pasta shells
6 cups shredded romaine lettuce
4 ounces alfalfa sprouts
1 8-ounce can water chestnuts,
thinly sliced
¼ ½ cup thinly sliced scallions
1 medium cucumber, thinly
sliced
3½ pounds (approximately 3–4
cups) cooked chicken, skinned,
boned, and cut into bite-size
pieces

1 6-ounce package frozen pea
pods, thawed
2½ ounces slivered almonds
French bread thinly sliced,
spread with cream cheese, and
sprinkled with minced parsley
(optional)

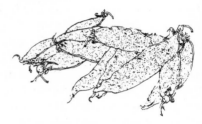

CURRIED MAYONNAISE DRESSING
2 cups mayonnaise, preferably
homemade (see page 181)
1 tablespoon curry powder
1½ tablespoons sugar

1 teaspoon ground ginger
1 tablespoon lemon juice
1½ teaspoons coarsely ground
black pepper

To prepare Curried Mayonnaise Dressing: In a medium bowl, mix all ingredients together until well blended. Set aside.

Cook pasta shells following directions on page 26. Drain into colander and set aside.

In a large, clear glass salad bowl, layer in order: lettuce, alfalfa sprouts, water chestnuts, scallions, cucumber, chicken, pea pods, and shells.

Spread Curried Mayonnaise Dressing over top, thoroughly covering layered ingredients. Cover with clear plastic wrap and refrigerate up to 24 hours. Just before serving, sprinkle almonds on top and toss to mix.

If desired, serve with thin slices of French bread spread with cream cheese and sprinkled with parsley.

Makes 8–10 generous servings.

DOUBLE-QUICK PASTA PRIMAVERA

This salad can be put together in a matter of minutes.

Vinaigrette Dressing with Herbs (see below)
1 10-ounce package frozen mixed vegetables
8 ounces ziti or other pasta shape
1 tablespoon peanut or vegetable oil
1 teaspoon salt

½ cup trimmed and chopped radishes
2–3 stalks celery, trimmed and cut into ½-inch julienne strips
½ cup chopped pitted black olives
Thin bread and butter sandwiches (optional)

VINAIGRETTE DRESSING WITH HERBS
2 teaspoons Dijon mustard
2 tablespoons red wine vinegar
1 teaspoon sugar
Salt
Coarsely ground black pepper

¼ cup mild virgin olive oil
Fresh herbs: minced parsley, snipped fresh chives, chopped watercress or basil leaves, etc.

To prepare Vinaigrette Dressing with Herbs: In medium bowl, combine mustard, vinegar, sugar, 1 teaspoon of salt, and 1 teaspoon of pepper. Whisk until blended and smooth. Slowly add oil, beating as added. When smooth, stir in herbs; if necessary, adjust seasoning with additional salt and pepper. Let stand at room temperature until ready to use. Beat to reblend just before using. Makes about ¾ cup.

Unwrap frozen vegetables and spread out on a large plate; let stand 10–15 minutes or until partially thawed.

Bring a large pot of water to a full boil and add ziti, oil, and salt. Stir once, then let water return to a full rolling boil. Boil for about 5 minutes, then add vegetables and continue to boil until pasta is *al dente* and vegetables are crisp cooked. Drain mixture into colander. Blot dry with paper toweling and transfer to a large bowl. Add radishes, celery, and olives. Pour Vinaigrette Dressing with Herbs over surface and toss to mix thoroughly. Can be refrigerated, covered, until about 30 minutes before serving. Serve at room temperature.

If desired, serve with thin bread and butter sandwiches.

Makes 4–6 servings.

FRUITED ORZO SALAD WITH FRESH VEGETABLES

What could be easier? Prepare the fruit and vegetables ahead, and refrigerate until ready to use. Cook and add the orzo. Serve and enjoy.

½ cup (approximately 2 ounces) diced mixed dried fruit
1 small zucchini
1 small yellow squash
Salt
1 small green pepper, finely chopped
½ cup cracked green olives, cut into slivers

3 tablespoons peanut or vegetable oil
1 small clove garlic, minced
1 teaspoon sugar
3 tablespoons white wine vinegar
¼ teaspoon coarsely ground black pepper
8 ounces orzo
Crisp lettuce leaves

Soak diced dried fruit overnight in enough water to cover. Drain thoroughly and blot dry. Place in a bowl. Set aside.

Trim and finely chop the zucchini and squash. Place into colander and sprinkle with 1 teaspoon of salt. Toss lightly to mix. Let stand at room temperature about 30 minutes, rinse, drain, and blot dry with paper toweling. Add to dried fruit. Add green pepper and olives. Toss to mix.

Pour oil into a small, heavy skillet and place over low heat. Add garlic and cook, stirring, until limp. Add sugar and stir until dissolved. Remove from heat. Stir in vinegar, 1 teaspoon of salt, and pepper. Whisk with fork until blended. Pour over fruit-vegetable mixture. If desired, cover and refrigerate until about 30 minutes before serving.

Cook orzo following directions on page 26. Drain into colander. Add to fruit-vegetable mixture. Toss lightly to mix.

Line individual salad plates or a serving bowl with lettuce. Top with salad.

Makes 6 servings.

GREEN NOODLE SALAD WITH CREAM CHEESE VEGETABLE DRESSING

This one is great for dieters but not only.

Cream Cheese Vegetable Dressing (see below)
8 ounces flat green noodles

1 tablespoon peanut or vegetable oil
¼ cup minced parsley

CREAM CHEESE VEGETABLE DRESSING
½ cup lowfat cottage cheese
¼ cup plain yogurt
¼ cup lowfat skim milk
2 tablespoons lemon juice
1 small tart apple, peeled, seeded, and chopped
¼ cup trimmed and chopped radishes
½ cup chopped green pepper
1 teaspoon paprika, preferably imported Hungarian hot paprika
Salt to taste

Prepare the Cream Cheese Vegetable Dressing: Place the cottage cheese, yogurt, skim milk, and lemon juice in the bowl of a food processor or blender; process or blend until smooth. Transfer the mixture to a medium bowl. Stir in the apple, radishes, green pepper, and paprika. Season to taste with salt. Set aside.

Cook noodles following directions on page 26. Drain into colander and transfer to a large bowl. Add oil, parsley, and Cream Cheese Vegetable Dressing and toss to mix. If desired, cover and refrigerate salad until about 30 minutes before serving. Transfer to a decorative bowl and sprinkle with parsley.

Makes 4 servings.

INLANDER'S PASTA SALAD WITH SEAFOOD

With frozen fish and shrimp from your freezer plus a can of minced clams from the kitchen shelf, you can prepare this salad for unexpected guests in a matter of minutes.

1 6½–7-ounce can minced clams
1 pound frozen filet of sole, individually separated
1 6–8-ounce package frozen, cooked, peeled, and deveined tiny bay shrimp
1 cup chopped celery
1 small green pepper, chopped

Curried Sour Cream Dressing (see below)
8 ounces bucatini or other small pasta shape
1 tablespoon large imported Italian capers, drained and chopped
Crisp lettuce leaves

CURRIED SOUR CREAM DRESSING
1 tablespoon lemon juice
½ teaspoon curry powder
½ teaspoon sugar

Salt to taste
1 cup sour cream or plain yogurt

Drain liquid from the can of clams into a large, heavy skillet; reserve clams. Add sufficient water to clam liquid to come to a depth of about 2 inches and bring to a boil. Add frozen filet of sole in a single layer and let simmer until opaque and firm through center. Use a slotted spatula to transfer the filets to paper toweling. Drain and blot dry with additional paper toweling. Break up into bite-size chunks and transfer to a large bowl. Place frozen shrimp into colander and rinse under hot water until thawed; blot thoroughly dry, then add to fish. Add reserved clams, celery, and green pepper.

To prepare Curried Sour Cream Dressing: In a small bowl, combine lemon juice, curry powder, and sugar and stir until curry powder has dissolved. Add sour cream and salt to taste; stir to mix thoroughly.

Cook bucatini following directions on page 26. Drain into colander, then add to seafood mixture in bowl. Stir in capers, add Curried Sour Cream Dressing, and toss to mix. Can be refrigerated, covered, until ready to serve. Transfer to a lettuce-lined bowl.

If desired, serve with Tomatoes with Capers and Parsley (see page 163).

Makes 4–6 servings.

Linguine Salad with Broccoli and Anchovy Sauce

Fast, inexpensive, but filled with great flavor.

1½–2 pounds broccoli
    8 ounces linguine or other thin
        pasta
    2 teaspoons peanut or vegeta-
        ble oil
    Extra-virgin olive oil
    1 2-ounce can flat anchovy
        filets, drained
    1 clove garlic, minced
    ½ teaspoon hot pepper flakes
    ¼ teaspoon coarsely ground
        black pepper
    2 tablespoons red wine vine-
        gar

Cut broccoli flowerets from stalks. Break large flowerets into bite-size pieces. Trim stalks and cut lengthwise into narrow (1½–2-inch) strips. Place stalks and flowerets in a large bowl of cold water. Let stand about 30 seconds, then drain off water. Bring a large pot of water to a full boil and add broccoli flowerets. Cook about 1 minute, then drain into colander and blot dry. Set aside.

Cook linguine following directions on page 26. Drain into colander, then transfer to a large bowl. Stir in peanut oil.

Pour ¼ cup of olive oil into a large pot over low heat. When hot, stir in anchovies and mash with a fork until blended. Add garlic, pepper flakes, and black pepper. Stir in broccoli and cook, stirring, for 2–3 minutes or until coated with sauce mixture. Remove from heat and stir in vinegar. Pour mixture over pasta. Toss to mix, adding additional oil if necessary.

Makes 4 servings.

VERMICELLI SALAD WITH RED PEPPER AND ZUCCHINI

Serve this easy-to-prepare but elegant salad as the first course of a seated dinner or as a main-course luncheon dish.

¼ cup peanut or vegetable oil
1 small clove garlic, crushed
1–2 large sweet red bell peppers, seeded and cut into julienne strips
1–2 (about 1 pound total weight) small zucchini, trimmed and cut into julienne strips

2 teaspoons sugar
2 tablespoons red or white wine vinegar
1–2 teaspoons soy sauce
8 ounces vermicelli or other very thin pasta strands
Toasted sesame seeds (optional)

Several hours or a day ahead, pour oil into a large, heavy skillet over medium heat. Add garlic and cook, stirring, until limp. Remove and discard garlic. Add pepper and zucchini strips; cook, stirring frequently, until very tender and limp. Stir in sugar; when dissolved, add vinegar. Remove skillet from heat and stir in soy sauce. Transfer to a storage bowl and refrigerate for several hours or overnight. Remove from refrigerator about 30 minutes before using.

Cook vermicelli following directions on page 26. Drain and place in a large bowl. Add zucchini-pepper mixture. Toss to mix thoroughly. Ladle onto large salad plates or into shallow soup bowls. If desired, sprinkle with toasted sesame seeds. Serve, if you like, with Italian bread sticks.

Makes 6 servings.

CAPELVENERE WITH SCALLOPS, SHRIMP, AND MEXICAN SALSA

Salsa in Spanish simply means sauce, but in this country it has come to mean a hot, spicy, uncooked tomato mixture. When teamed with seafood and capelvenere it becomes an unbeatable combination.

Salsa (uncooked tomato sauce; see below)
½ cup dry white wine or vermouth
1½ cups water
1 bay leaf
4–6 black peppercorns
1 sprig parsley
1 sprig fresh thyme, or ½ teaspoon dried thyme
1 small white onion, thinly sliced

Lemon wedge
1 clove garlic, crushed (optional)
1 teaspoon salt
1 pound fresh scallops (leave small scallops whole; cut large scallops into halves or fourths)
1 pound raw shrimp, peeled and deveined
8 ounces capelvenere
Minced parsley for garnish (optional)

SALSA
3 large sun-ripened tomatoes
4–6 ripe olives, pitted and finely chopped
1 teaspoon minced garlic
1 small, hot red pepper, minced
¼ cup minced coriander leaves or parsley flakes

1 teaspoon salt
Juice of 1 medium-size lime
2–3 tablespoons mild virgin olive oil

To prepare Salsa: Hold tomatoes one at a time over a large bowl and cut into bite-size chunks, letting chunks and juice fall into bowl. Add olives, garlic, pepper, and coriander. Stir in salt, lime juice, and olive oil. Let stand at room temperature until ready to use.

In a large saucepan, combine wine, water, bay leaf, peppercorns, parsley, thyme, onion, lemon wedge, and garlic, if desired. Season with salt. Place over medium heat and let simmer about 30 minutes. Strain and return liquid to saucepan, discarding solids. Add scallops, cover, and simmer 3–4 minutes. Remove pot from heat and let scallops cool to room temperature, then scoop them out and place in a medium bowl.

Return the liquid to heat and bring to a boil. Add shrimp. Let cook at a brisk simmer for 3–4 minutes or until firm and pink. Add shrimp to scallops with about ½ cup of the broth. Cover and refrigerate until ready to use.

Cook capelvenere following directions on page 26. Drain into colander, then transfer to a large bowl. Drain scallops and shrimp and add to bowl. Toss to mix. Transfer to large salad plates or shallow bowls. Top each serving with Salsa and garnish with minced parsley, if desired. Serve at room temperature.

Makes 4–6 servings.

LINGUINE WITH UNCOOKED TOMATO SAUCE

Prepare this salad midsummer when there's an abundance of sun-ripened tomatoes and fresh herbs in your garden.

3 large sun-ripened tomatoes
½ cup chopped fresh basil leaves
¼ cup minced parsley
¼ cup minced chives
¼ cup drained capers
8 ounces Brie cheese, with rind removed and torn into bite-size pieces
½ cup mild, fruity virgin olive oil
2 tablespoons tarragon vinegar
1 teaspoon sugar
Generous sprinkling of coarsely ground black pepper
Salt to taste
12 ounces linguine
½ cup grated Parmesan cheese

Two to 3 hours ahead: Hold tomatoes one at a time over a large bowl and cut into bite-size chunks, letting chunks and juice fall into bowl. Add basil, parsley, and chives. Stir in capers and Brie cheese. Add oil, vinegar, and sugar. Season generously with pepper and add salt to taste. Set aside at room temperature.

Cook linguine following directions on page 26. Drain into colander, then add to tomato mixture while still hot. Add Parmesan cheese and toss to combine ingredients thoroughly.

Makes 4–6 servings.

Macaroni Salad New York–Style

This recipe is from a Lower East Side delicatessen in Manhattan famous for its hearty pastrami sandwiches as well as its "home-style" herring.

1 8-ounce jar herring filets in
    cream
¼ cup chopped sweet gherkins
1 medium-size red onion, chopped
2 medium-size tart, crisp, un-
    peeled apples, cored, seeded,
    and chopped

1 8-ounce carton sour cream
1 tablespoon spicy mustard
8 ounces mezzani or other short,
    cut macaroni
    Salt to taste
    Minced fresh dill for garnish
    (optional)

Remove herring from jar and cut into small dice. Place in a large bowl and add the cream from the jar. Add gherkins, onion, and apples.

In a small bowl, combine sour cream and mustard. Pour over herring mixture. Set aside.

Cook mezzani following directions on page 26. Drain into colander, then add to salad. Can be refrigerated, covered, until about 30 minutes before serving. Transfer to a serving bowl, salt to taste, and, if you like, sprinkle evenly with minced dill.

If desired, serve with split and buttered rye deli rolls.

Makes 6–8 servings.

MACARONI SALAD WITH OLIVE DRESSING

For the simplest of all menus, serve this salad with thick slices of Italian-style bread, a crock of sweet butter, a wedge of Brie or Camembert cheese, and sliced sun-ripened tomatoes. A light red wine is the perfect accompaniment.

1 8-ounce jar pitted green olives, drained and chopped

1 cup chopped pitted Niçoise olives

1 small (4-ounce) jar pimiento strips, drained

2 tablespoons capers

¼ cup minced Italian parsley

½ cup olive oil

3 tablespoons red wine vinegar

1 teaspoon oregano

Coarsely ground black pepper to taste

8 ounces bucatini

1 cup shredded iceberg lettuce

4 ounces Genoa salami, thinly sliced and cut into narrow strips

4 ounces mozzarella cheese, thinly sliced and cut into narrow strips

Several hours or a day ahead: In a large non-metal bowl, combine olives, pimiento strips, capers, and parsley. Add oil, vinegar, and oregano. Toss to mix ingredients. Stir in pepper to taste. Cover bowl and refrigerate. Bring to room temperature before using.

Cook bucatini following directions on page 26. Drain into colander, then add to olive mixture. Stir in lettuce, salami, and mozzarella. Toss ingredients to mix thoroughly.

Makes 6–8 servings.

LEMONY MEZZANI SALAD

Prepare the mayonnaise a day ahead if you like. Then cook the pasta and toss with mayonnaise and remaining ingredients.

Lemony Mayonnaise (see below)
1 pound mezzani
4 ounces tender young spinach leaves, torn into bite-size pieces
2 tablespoons chopped shallots
2 tablespoons chopped watercress leaves

2 tablespoons chopped parsley
1 tablespoon fresh tarragon leaves, chopped (optional)
4 ounces Genoa salami, cut into narrow strips
10–12 cherry tomatoes, rinsed, blotted dry, and halved

LEMONY MAYONNAISE
1 large egg
Pinch of dry mustard
Salt
Freshly squeezed lemon juice
⅓ cup mild virgin olive oil
⅓ cup vegetable oil

To prepare Lemony Mayonnaise: Place egg, mustard, ½ teaspoon of salt, and 2 tablespoons of lemon juice in the bowl of a food processor or blender. Process or blend until smooth. With motor running, slowly add olive oil. When mixture begins to thicken, add vegetable oil in a steady stream and mix until smooth. Taste for seasoning. Add more salt or lemon juice if desired. Transfer to a storage bowl, cover, and refrigerate until ready to use. Set aside.

Cook mezzani following directions on page 26. Drain into colander, then transfer to a large bowl. Add Lemony Mayonnaise and remaining ingredients. Toss to mix. If desired, cover and refrigerate until about 30 minutes before serving. Serve at room temperature.

Makes 6 servings.

VERMICELLI SALAD WITH SESAME DRESSING

You can make this salad several hours or a day before serving.

8 ounces vermicelli
1 tablespoon sesame oil
¼ cup minced scallions
2 tablespoons minced parsley
3 tablespoons peanut or vegetable oil
1 tablespoon sugar

1 tablespoon imported black soy sauce
1 tablespoon dark Chinese vinegar
2 teaspoons Oriental hot pepper oil
½ tablespoon salt

Several hours or a day ahead: Cook pasta following directions on page 26. Drain into colander and rinse well under cold running water. Blot dry and transfer to a large bowl. Add sesame oil, scallions, and parsley. Toss to mix. Set aside.

Pour peanut oil into a large, heavy skillet over medium heat and stir in sugar. Remove skillet from heat and stir in soy sauce, vinegar, hot pepper oil, and salt. Cool slightly, then pour over noodle mixture. Toss with 2 forks to distribute ingredients thoroughly. Cover and refrigerate. Let stand at room temperature about 30 minutes before serving.

If desired, serve with Tomato Sandwich Rounds (see page 168).

Makes 4 servings.

SHANGHAI-STYLE NOODLE SALAD

A flavorful mix of textures and tastes.

6 tablespoons mild virgin olive oil

3 tablespoons peanut or vegetable oil

3 tablespoons white wine vinegar

1 tablespoon chopped fresh tarragon leaves, or ¼ teaspoon dried tarragon

½ teaspoon sugar (optional)

1 teaspoon salt or to taste

¼ teaspoon coarsely ground black pepper or to taste

1 large clove garlic, crushed

2 6-ounce packages peeled and deveined frozen popcorn (tiny) shrimp

1 cup fresh or frozen green peas

6-8 water chestnuts, chopped

½ cup minced green onions

4-5 ounces thin Chinese wheat noodles

In a medium bowl, combine olive oil, peanut oil, vinegar, tarragon, sugar, salt, and pepper. Whisk until blended, then add garlic. Set dressing aside for about 1 hour, or cover and refrigerate for several hours. Remove and discard garlic. Pour dressing into a large salad bowl. Set aside.

Place shrimp and peas into large colander. Rinse under very hot water until shrimp are thawed. Drain thoroughly and blot dry. Add to dressing in salad bowl. Add water chestnuts and green onions.

Place noodles in a large heat-proof bowl and cover with about 2 inches of boiling water. Let stand 3-4 minutes, then lift and separate strands with a fork. Let stand 3-4 minutes more or until tender. Drain into colander, then blot thoroughly dry. Add to salad bowl mixture. Toss to mix. Serve at room temperature.

Makes 6-8 servings.

CHINATOWN VERMICELLI SALAD

I've known about Chinese vermicelli for only a few years, while in China they have been used for more than a century. Why didn't someone tell me? They're delicious and especially great for salad making.

1 large green bell pepper
10–12 radishes
1 cup mung bean sprouts
4–5 ounces thin Chinese vermicelli
6 tablespoons peanut or vegetable oil
1 tablespoon Oriental sesame oil
3 tablespoons rice wine vinegar
¼ cup minced green onions
2 tablespoons minced parsley
Salt and pepper to taste

Cut green peppers lengthwise into quarters; remove all seeds and white ribs. Cut lengthwise into narrow strips. Wash, trim, and slice radishes. Place both vegetables in a large heat-proof bowl. Bring a large pot of water to a full boil. Pour over vegetables and let stand about 1 minute. Pour off water and blot vegetables dry, then transfer them to a large salad bowl.

Place bean sprouts in the same heat-proof bowl. If necessary, bring more water to a full boil, pour over sprouts, and let stand about 1 minute. Loose hulls will float to the top; gently pour them off, then drain sprouts into colander and blot dry. Add to pepper-radish mixture.

Place vermicelli in the same heat-proof bowl and again bring a large pot of water to a full boil. Pour over vermicelli and let stand 3–4 minutes, then lift and separate strands with a fork. Let stand 3–4 minutes more or until tender. Pour off water, blot dry, and add to vegetable mixture.

In a small bowl, combine peanut oil and sesame oil. Add vinegar and whisk until smooth. Stir in green onions and parsley. Season to taste with salt and pepper. Pour over vegetable-vermicelli mixture. Toss to mix. Serve at room temperature.

Makes 6 servings.

PASTA RUSTICA

This is a great salad to prepare for large picnic-style outings or poolside buffet parties. It's enough for 10–12 servings, but even when prepared for 6–8 guests there's never enough left even for tomorrow's lunch.

2 tablespoons peanut or vegetable oil

2 medium-size carrots, scraped and cut at a 45-degree angle into thin oval slices

1 medium zucchini, trimmed and cut into ¼-inch slices

1 large onion, chopped

½ cup thinly sliced radishes

¼ cup minced parsley

2–3 tablespoons minced fresh basil leaves

1 cup shredded Chinese cabbage

or bok choy

1 15-ounce can cannellini beans

1 tablespoon light fruity olive oil, or 1 tablespoon peanut or vegetable oil

1 tablespoon white wine vinegar

1 teaspoon salt
Coarsely ground black pepper to taste
Anchovy Mayonnaise (see below)

12 ounces rigatoni

ANCHOVY MAYONNAISE

1 cup thick mayonnaise, store-bought or homemade (see page 181)

1 tablespoon anchovy paste or fortified minced anchovy filets

3–4 tablespoons lemon juice

Pour oil into a large heavy skillet over medium heat. When hot, add carrots and stir-fry about 1 minute. Add zucchini, onion, and radishes. Cook, stirring, about 2 minutes. Scrape mixture into a large bowl. Add parsley, basil, shredded cabbage, and beans. Stir in olive oil and vinegar. Season with salt and pepper. Toss ingredients to mix. Set aside.

To prepare Anchovy Mayonnaise: Combine all ingredients in a small bowl. Stir to mix and, if desired, cover and refrigerate until ready to use.

Cook pasta following directions on page 26. Drain into colander and, while still warm, add to vegetable mixture. Toss lightly to mix ingredients. Stir in Anchovy Mayonnaise. If desired, cover and refrigerate for several hours or overnight. Bring to room temperature before serving.

Makes 10–12 medium-size servings or 6–8 large servings.

PASTA SALAD WITH ASPARAGUS

Because the asparagus are stir-fried instead of steamed or boiled, their bright green color is retained and they are tenderized in a matter of seconds. The ham and shrimp add both color and flavor, and the water chestnuts give crunch. All in all, it's a festive salad.

Soy Vinaigrette (see below)
1 pound asparagus
1 tablespoon peanut or vegetable oil
1 small clove garlic, crushed
1 1-inch square fresh ginger root, trimmed and crushed
8 ounces medium-size shrimp, peeled and deveined

¼ cup water
4 ounces baked Virginia ham, cut into julienne strips
6–8 canned water chestnuts, thinly sliced
6–8 large California olives, pitted and sliced
8 ounces fedelini or linguine

SOY VINAIGRETTE
1 tablespoon soy sauce
2 tablespoons white wine vinegar

Pinch of dry mustard
6 tablespoons peanut or vegetable oil
Salt and pepper to taste

To prepare Soy Vinaigrette: Combine soy sauce and vinegar in a small bowl. Stir in mustard. Slowly add oil, beating as added. Season to taste with salt and pepper. Set aside.

Break tough ends from asparagus. Wash briefly under cold running water. Blot dry and roll-cut (see directions below) into 1-inch pieces. In a large saucepan or wok, heat oil over medium heat. Add garlic and ginger and stir until garlic is limp. Remove and discard garlic and ginger. Add asparagus and shrimp and stir rapidly to coat with oil. Pour in water, cover, and steam 2–3 minutes until asparagus are just tender and shrimp are firm and pink. Uncover, turn up heat, and cook 1 minute more, stirring to evaporate any liquid. Remove from heat and transfer asparagus and shrimp to a large bowl. Add ham, water chestnuts, and olives. Stir in Soy Vinaigrette and set aside.

Cook pasta following directions on page 26. Drain into colander. Add while still warm to asparagus mixture and toss to incorporate ingredients completely.

Makes 6 servings.

HOW TO ROLL-CUT ASPARAGUS
This method of cutting vegetables exposes a greater cut surface area to the heat, allowing the vegetable to absorb additional flavor from the other ingredients. Start at the end of the trimmed asparagus spear; make a diagonal cut, roll asparagus a quarter turn, and make another diagonal cut; continue rolling and cutting down the spear until you have several diamond-shaped pieces.

ROTELLE WITH MARINATED EGGPLANT

Serve this Mediterranean-style salad with split and toasted small pita bread rounds. Brush them with fruity olive oil, then cut into pie-shaped wedges.

1 pound firm, fresh eggplant	1 tablespoon dried basil
Coarse salt	Coarsely ground black pep-
1 cup light, fruity olive oil	per to taste
3 tablespoons red wine vine-	Salt to taste
gar	8 ounces rotelle
¼ teaspoon Tabasco sauce	12–16 small cherry tomatoes,
2 cloves garlic, minced	halved and seeded
1 tablespoon dried oregano	¼ cup minced parsley

Two or 3 days ahead: Trim unpeeled eggplant and cut into ½-inch cubes. Place cubes into large colander and sprinkle heavily with coarse salt (about 1 tablespoon). Toss cubes with your hands to coat them evenly. Cover them directly with a large, heavy plate that will just fit inside colander. Let stand about 1 hour. Rinse under cold running water, then transfer to double-thick paper toweling. Blot dry with additional paper toweling. Transfer to a large bowl.

In a small bowl, combine oil, vinegar, and Tabasco sauce. Stir in garlic, oregano, and basil. Sprinkle heavily with pepper and very lightly with salt, if desired. Pour mixture over eggplant cubes. Cover bowl and refrigerate, stirring cubes occasionally.

When ready to prepare, drain marinade from eggplant (if desired, reserve marinade for other use).

Cook rotelle following directions on page 26. Drain into colander and add to eggplant. Add cherry tomatoes and parsley and toss to mix ingredients thoroughly. Cover and refrigerate salad, if you like, but bring to room temperature before serving.

If desired, serve with Toasted Pita Bread with Tahini (see recipe page 168).

Makes 6 servings.

MEZZANI SALAD MEDITERRANEAN-STYLE

This salad looks positively beautiful on a buffet luncheon table.

1 2-ounce can flat anchovy filets,
  drained
1 6–8-ounce can tuna
½ cup thinly sliced celery
1 small green pepper, seeded and
  cut into narrow strips
1 large ripe tomato, halved,
  seeded, and cut into narrow
  strips

½ cup minced parsley
¼ cup minced chives or green
  onions
  Creamy Vinaigrette Dressing
  (see below)
8 ounces mezzani
  Pitted Niçoise olives, tomato
  wedges, and hard-cooked egg
  wedges for garnish

CREAMY VINAIGRETTE DRESSING
2 tablespoons white wine vinegar
⅓ cup mild fruity olive oil
4 tablespoons thick mayonnaise,
  preferably homemade (see page
  181)
  Salt to taste
  Coarsely ground black pepper
  to taste

Place anchovies in a large bowl and cut into small pieces. Add tuna and break up with a fork. Add celery, green pepper, and tomato. Stir in parsley and chives. Set aside.

To prepare Creamy Vinaigrette Dressing: Combine vinegar and olive oil in a small bowl. Stir in mayonnaise and season with salt and pepper.

Cook mezzani following directions on page 26. Drain into colander, then, while still warm, add to tuna mixture. Toss lightly. Let stand about 15 minutes. Stir in Creamy Vinaigrette Dressing. Transfer salad to a large serving bowl. If desired, garnish with olives, tomato wedges, and hard-cooked egg wedges.

Makes 8–10 servings.

MIDSUMMER PASTA SALAD

These flavors and colors come together to create a memorable salad.

2 small zucchini, trimmed and
  diced
½ medium-size purple onion,
  peeled and chopped
1 small cucumber, peeled, seeded,
  and diced
2 large sun-ripened tomatoes,
  peeled, seeded, and chopped
2 tablespoons capers
½ cup chopped fresh basil leaves

½ cup fruity olive oil
2 tablespoons red wine vinegar
  Salt to taste
  Coarsely ground black pepper
  to taste
8 ounces rigatoni
4 ounces mozzarella cheese,
  coarsely grated or finely
  chopped

In a large bowl, combine zucchini, onion, cucumber, and tomatoes. Stir in capers and basil leaves. Add oil and vinegar. Toss to mix, then season to taste with salt and pepper.

Cook rigatoni following directions on page 26. Drain into colander. Add to vegetable mixture and stir in cheese.

If desired, serve with buttered croissants.

Makes 6 servings.

SPAGHETTINI AND GREEN BEAN SALAD GRUYÈRE

The perfect main-course salad for a hot summer evening, serve this one with thin bread and flavored butter sandwiches (see pp. 164–65) and a chilled white wine.

8 ounces crisp, young green snap
  beans
Salt
½ cup light olive oil
1 teaspoon sugar
1 teaspoon salt or to taste
2 tablespoons sherry wine vinegar

1 tablespoon Dijon mustard
8 ounces spaghettini
¼ cup chopped Italian parsley
8 ounces large mushrooms,
  trimmed and thinly sliced
4 ounces Gruyère cheese,
  coarsely grated

Several hours or a day ahead: Cook green beans in a large pot of rapidly boiling salted water until crisp-tender. Drain into colander and transfer to a large bowl.

Pour oil into a large, heavy skillet over low heat. Add sugar and salt and stir until sugar has dissolved. Cool slightly, then add vinegar and mustard. Taste, then add additional salt if desired. Pour over beans. Cover and refrigerate. Remove from refrigerator and bring to room temperature before using.

Cook pasta following directions on page 26. Drain into colander and add to bean mixture. Add parsley, mushrooms, and cheese, then toss to mix.

Makes 6–8 servings.

Fettuccine with Seafood and Basil Cream Dressing

Here is a spectacular main-course salad, just perfect for a buffet luncheon or supper party. Easy on the hostess-cook because it can and should be made 1 or even 2 days ahead to allow flavors to mellow and blend.

Vinaigrette Dressing (see below)
Basil Cream Dressing (see below)
1 pound fettuccine, broken into 1–2-inch pieces
12–16 very thin asparagus spears
1 small bunch broccoli
1 10-ounce package tiny green peas, thawed
4 tablespoons peanut or vegetable oil

2 cloves garlic, crushed
1–1½ pounds bay scallops, cut across into 2 or 3 slices
2 pounds medium or large shrimp, peeled and deveined
16–18 small cherry tomatoes, halved and seeded
Crisp spinach leaves
¼ cup minced chives

VINAIGRETTE DRESSING
6 tablespoons fruity olive oil
2 tablespoons red wine vinegar

Salt and pepper to taste

BASIL CREAM DRESSING
¼ cup white wine vinegar
1 tablespoon Dijon or similar mustard
¼ cup minced fresh basil leaves, or 3 tablespoons dried basil

1 tablespoon vegetable oil
1 cup sour cream
¼ cup minced fresh parsley
Salt to taste
Coarsely ground black pepper to taste

To prepare Vinaigrette Dressing: Combine oil and vinegar in a small bowl. Beat until blended. Season with salt and pepper to taste.

To prepare Basil Cream Dressing: Combine vinegar, mustard, and basil in the bowl of a food processor or blender; process until mixed. With machine running, drizzle in oil. Add sour cream and parsley; process until well blended. Season to taste with salt and pepper. Cover and refrigerate until just before using. Reblend before transferring to serving bowl.

Cook fettuccine following directions on page 26. Drain into colander and transfer to a large bowl. Add about 2 tablespoons of Vinaigrette Dressing and toss to mix. Set aside.

Trim asparagus and cut across into 1–1½-inch lengths. Break broccoli flowerets from stems and break large flowerets into bite-size pieces. Trim and cut stems into ½-inch strips. Place frozen peas into colander to drain.

Pour 2 tablespoons of oil into a large, heavy skillet over low heat; add 1 crushed clove garlic and stir until limp. Remove and discard garlic. Raise heat to high. Add broccoli stems and stir-fry about 1 minute. Add broccoli flowerets and asparagus and stir-fry about 30 seconds. With a slotted spoon transfer vegetables to a medium bowl, cover with remaining Vinaigrette Dressing, and stir in peas. Cover bowl and refrigerate until ready to use.

Pour remaining oil into a skillet and add remaining garlic. Stir-fry about 30 seconds; remove and discard garlic. Add scallops and shrimp; stir-fry until scallops are firm and shrimp are pink, 3–4 minutes. Drain into colander, then add to fettuccine. If desired, cover and refrigerate until ready to complete salad.

Just before serving, drain and add vegetable mixture to fettuccine mixture. Add cherry tomato halves and toss salad again to mix ingredients thoroughly.

Arrange spinach leaves around edge of a large round or oblong platter. Spoon salad into center of platter and sprinkle with chives. Serve Basil Cream Dressing separately.

Makes 8–12 large servings or 12–16 small servings as part of a buffet supper.

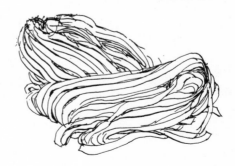

VERMICELLI WITH FILET OF SOLE AND SUN-DRIED TOMATOES

Ordinarily we prefer fresh to frozen seafood, but frozen, individually wrapped filet of sole is an excellent alternative for this salad.

4–6 ounce jar sun-dried tomato halves

¼ cup oil from jar of sun-dried tomatoes

¼ cup peanut or vegetable oil

1 tablespoon white wine or tarragon vinegar

¼ teaspoon coarsely ground black pepper

½ cup chopped celery

¼ cup minced parsley

¼ cup chopped alfonso olives

Juice of 1 small lemon

½ teaspoon salt

1 pound fresh filet of sole, or 1-pound package frozen, individually wrapped filet of sole

8 ounces vermicelli

Drain oil from tomatoes into a measuring cup and add peanut oil. Pour into a large bowl. Stir in vinegar and add pepper. Using a very sharp knife, cut tomatoes into narrow strips and add to oil mixture. Stir in celery, parsley, and olives. Set aside.

Fill a large, heavy skillet with water to a depth of about 2 inches. Add lemon juice and salt. Bring to a brisk simmer, then add fish in a single layer. Let the fish cook, uncovered, until white and opaque through the center. Transfer to paper toweling to drain briefly. Break into large chunks and add to the bowl with tomato mixture.

Cook pasta following directions on page 26. Drain into colander, cool slightly, and add to tomato-fish mixture. Toss salad and serve at room temperature.

Makes 6 servings.

ROTELLE WITH FRESH HERBS

This is a favorite pasta salad for a sunny midsummer day. The warm vinaigrette dressing and still-hot pasta bring out the flavor of the fresh herbs in a wonderfully subtle way. Yet it is quick to prepare and delicious.

½ cup coarsely chopped fresh
  herbs, stems removed (use
  chives, parsley, basil, and oregano, or any herbs available in
  your garden or at your grocer)
⅓ cup virgin or extra-virgin olive
  oil
2 tablespoons white wine, basil,
  or other herb-flavored vinegar
½ teaspoon salt
½ teaspoon dried, hot pepper
  flakes
12 ounces rotelle
½ cup grated Parmesan cheese

Place herbs in a large serving bowl. Pour oil into a small skillet over low heat. When very hot, but before it begins to smoke, pour over herbs. Stir in vinegar, salt, and hot pepper flakes. Set aside at room temperature.

Cook pasta folloowing directions on page 26. Drain into colander, then add the pasta to the herb mixture while still warm. Add cheese and toss to mix. Serve at room temperature.

If desired, serve with Chicken, Shrimp, or Tuna Sandwiches (see page 171).

Makes 4 servings.

RIGATONI WITH TOMATOES AND SALSA VERDE

Salsa verde is a sharp, uncooked green sauce. It is to Latin America what pesto sauce is to Italy.

1 2-ounce can anchovies with capers, drained
1 small hot green chili pepper, seeded and minced
1 small clove garlic, chopped
Lemon juice
½ cup (loosely packed) minced parsley
Extra-virgin olive oil

2 large sun-ripened tomatoes, peeled, seeded, and diced
Coarsely ground black pepper to taste
8 ounces rigatoni or other thin pasta
Crisp bread sticks, each rolled in a thin slice of prosciutto (optional)

Place anchovies, chili pepper, garlic, and 2 tablespoons of lemon juice in the bowl of a food processor. Process to a chunky paste. Add parsley. Gradually add 4 tablespoons of oil in a thin, steady stream. Taste and correct seasoning with additional lemon juice or oil, if desired. Stir in tomatoes. Add pepper to taste. Scrape mixture into a large bowl and set aside.

Cook pasta following directions on page 26. Drain into colander, then add to salsa mixture and toss to mix. Serve at room temperature.

If desired, serve with crisp bread sticks rolled in thin slices of prosciutto.

Makes 4 servings.

SHELLS WITH TUNA AND VEGETABLES

Here is a hearty salad full of satisfying flavors and textures.

1 7½-ounce can imported Italian tuna packed in olive oil
Peanut or vegetable oil, if needed
3 tablespoons red wine vinegar
1 teaspoon Dijon or similar mustard
1 teaspoon coarse salt
Coarsely ground black pepper

8 ounces fresh green snap beans
2 stalks celery, cut at a 45-degree angle into thin crescent shapes
1 small red bell pepper, seeded and cut into julienne strips
1 tablespoon capers
¼ cup minced Italian parsley
8 ounces small pasta shells

Drain oil from tuna and place in a measuring cup. If necessary, add sufficient peanut oil to measure ½ cup. Pour into a large bowl. Add vinegar, mustard, salt, and pepper. Break tuna into bite-size chunks and add to dressing mixture.

Trim beans. Cook in a large pot of rapidly boiling water until crisp-tender, 10–12 minutes. Drain into colander and rinse immediately under cold running water to stop cooking process. Place beans on a chopping board and cut into ½-inch pieces. Add to tuna mixture. Stir in celery, red pepper, capers, and parsley. Set aside at room temperature.

Cook pasta following directions on page 26. Drain into colander, then add to salad. Toss to mix thoroughly. Serve at room temperature.
Makes 4–6 servings.

Angelino's favorite

Because the vegetables are prepared a day ahead, all you need to do is cook the pasta, toss in the vegetables, and serve.

8 ounces green snap beans

1 1-pound can red kidney beans, drained and rinsed

1 6-ounce jar marinated artichoke hearts, drained with marinade reserved

½ cup chopped Niçoise olives

1 1½-ounce jar pickled mushrooms, drained

1 2-ounce jar pimiento strips, drained

1 tablespoon capers

Parsley

2 tablespoons minced green onion or chives

¼ cup mild virgin olive oil

1 tablespoon white wine vinegar

2 tablespoons marinade from artichokes

Sprinkling of crushed dry tarragon leaves

Pinch of cayenne pepper

Salt to taste

Coarsely ground black pepper to taste

12 ounces small pasta shapes

Several hours or a day ahead: Wash beans under cold running water and snip off ends. Place on steamer rack over simmering water; cover and steam until crisp-tender. Rinse immediately under cold running water and transfer to a large bowl. Add kidney beans, artichoke hearts, olives, mushrooms, pimientos, and capers. Stir in parsley, green onion, oil, vinegar, marinade from artichokes, tarragon, and cayenne pepper. Toss to mix ingredients thoroughly. Add salt and pepper to taste.

Cover bowl and refrigerate. Remove from refrigerator about 30 minutes before preparing pasta.

Cook pasta following directions on page 26. Drain into colander and, while still hot, add to vegetable mixture. Toss thoroughly. Serve at room temperature.

Makes 6–8 servings.

MEZZANI WITH WINTER VEGETABLES

For this salad, crisp, stir-fried vegetables are teamed upwith mezzani, Sicilian olives, and salami.

Sour Cream Mayonnaise (see below)
2 tablespoons peanut or vegetable oil
3 cloves garlic, crushed
2 medium-size carrots, scraped and cut at a 45-degree angle into thin, oval slices
1 cup broccoli flowerets
1 cup cauliflowerets

1 cup frozen green peas, thawed
½ cup thinly sliced celery
8 ounces mezzani
4 ounces hard salami, cut into narrow strips
½ cup Sicilian or other imported olives
1–2 tablespoons water-packed green peppercorns
Salt to taste

SOUR CREAM MAYONNAISE
1 cup mayonnaise, preferably homemade (see recipe page 181)
¼ cup sour cream
¼ cup Dijon or similar mustard

1 teaspoon dried tarragon
1 teaspoon dried basil
Salt to taste
Coarsely ground black pepper to taste

Prepare Sour Cream Mayonnaise by combining all ingredients. Mix well and set aside until ready to use.

Place oil in a large, heavy skillet or wok over low heat. Add garlic and cook, stirring frequently, until limp. Remove and discard garlic. Add carrots and stir-fry about 1 minute. Add broccoli and cauliflowerets. Stir-fry about 30 seconds. Stir in peas and celery. Continue to stir-fry for 30 seconds more. To remove oil, drain vegetables into colander. Transfer to a large bowl. Set aside.

Cook pasta following directions on page 26. Drain into colander, then add to vegetable mixture. Add salami, olives, green peppercorns, and salt to taste. Toss lightly to mix ingredients. Add Sour Cream Mayonnaise and toss gently but thoroughly. Cover salad until about 30 minutes before serving.

Makes 6 servings.

PASTA SALAD WITH SALMON

Here is a rich combination of red salmon, black olives, and crisp Belgian endive put together with an incredibly delicious but easy-to-prepare dressing.

Béarnaise Mayonnaise (see
  below)
1 1-pound can red (sockeye)
  salmon
2 medium-size Belgian endive,
  trimmed and sliced into thin
  rounds
3–4 stalks celery, cut at a 45-
  degree angle into thin crescent
  shapes
1 cup small fresh green peas or
  frozen green peas, thawed

¼ cup small capers
8 ounces pasta twists or shells
  Crisp lettuce leaves
  Thick slices crusty Italian
  bread (optional)

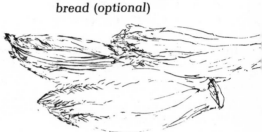

BÉARNAISE MAYONNAISE
2 shallots, minced
¼ cup dry white wine
¼ cup white wine vinegar
1 tablespoon dried tarragon
1 teaspoon dried dill

1 cup thick mayonnaise, preferably homemade (see page 181)
  Salt to taste
  Coarsely ground black pepper
  to taste

To prepare Béarnaise Mayonnaise: Place shallots, wine, vinegar, tarragon, and dill in a saucepan over medium heat. Let simmer until liquid is reduced to about 2 tablespoons. Pour into medium mixing bowl. Stir in mayonnaise and season to taste with salt and pepper. Cover and refrigerate until chilled.

Drain and place salmon in a large bowl; break up with a fork into small chunks. Add endive, celery, peas, and capers. Gently fold in Béarnaise Mayonnaise.

Cook pasta following directions on page 26. Drain into colander and add to salmon mixture. Cover salad and refrigerate to blend flavors for several hours or overnight. Spoon onto lettuce-lined salad plates.

If desired, serve with thick slices of crusty Italian bread.

Makes 6 servings.

CAPELLINI WITH GOURMET PESTO

You can now find commercially prepared pesto in gourmet-type food shops as well as many supermarkets. It makes a great midwinter substitute for homemade pesto sauce.

4 ounces bottled pesto
¼ cup grated Parmesan cheese
   About 1 tablespoon lemon juice or to taste
   About 4 tablespoons mild, fruity olive oil or to taste
1 small clove garlic, minced (optional)
¼ cup pine nuts or chopped almonds
12 ounces capellini

In a large bowl, combine pesto and Parmesan cheese. Stir in lemon juice and olive oil to taste. (Mixture should be medium thick.) If desired, add garlic. Stir in pine nuts. Set aside.

Cook capellini following directions on page 26. Drain into colander and, while still hot, add to basil pesto sauce. Toss to mix. Serve at room temperature.

If desired, serve with Marinated Cucumbers (see recipe page 158).
Makes 4–6 servings.

DITALI SALAD WITH RED AND GREEN PEPPERS

The distinctive flavor of stir-fried peppers, accented by a garlicky vinaigrette, gives this salad its outstanding taste.

3 green bell peppers
3 red bell peppers
3 tablespoons mild, fruity olive oil
3 cloves garlic, crushed
1 tablespoon sugar
2 tablespoons red wine vinegar
1 teaspoon dried oregano
1 tablespoon chopped fresh basil leaves, or 1 teaspoon dried basil
1 teaspoon coarse salt
8 ounces ditali (short macaroni)
½ cup chopped pitted Niçoise olives

Cut peppers lengthwise into quarters. Remove all seeds and white ribs. Slice into strips ½ inch wide.

Pour oil into a large, heavy skillet over low heat. Add garlic and cook, stirring, until limp. Remove and discard garlic. Add pepper strips and stir-fry until crisp-tender. Stir in sugar, vinegar, oregano, and basil. When sugar has dissolved, remove skillet from heat and scrape contents into a large bowl. Season with salt. Set aside at room temperature until ready to use.

Cook pasta following directions on page 26. Drain into colander and add to pepper mixture. Stir in olives. Serve warm.

Makes 6 servings.

MACARONI SALAD WITH SHRIMP AND CREAMY VINAIGRETTE

This makes an elegant luncheon salad for special guests.

4 ounces small macaroni
Peanut or vegetable oil
1 egg yolk
2 teaspoons Dijon or Dusseldorf-type mustard
1 teaspoon tarragon wine vinegar
2–3 dashes of Tabasco sauce
¼ teaspoon salt or to taste
2 tablespoons fresh lemon juice
1 pound cooked shrimp, peeled and deveined

1 cup finely chopped celery
1 tablespoon capers
1 tablespoon chopped fresh tarragon, or ½ teaspoon dried tarragon
1 tablespoon minced parsley
Crisp lettuce leaves
3 tablespoons finely diced green pepper

Cook pasta following directions on page 26. Drain into colander, then transfer to a bowl and stir in 2 teaspoons of oil. Set aside.

In a second large bowl, combine egg yolk, mustard, vinegar, Tabasco sauce, and salt. Whisk until blended. Gradually add ¼ cup of oil, whisking constantly. Whisk in lemon juice.

When the mixture is thick and smooth, add pasta, shrimp, celery, capers, tarragon, and parsley. Toss with 2 forks to mix. Spoon salad onto 4 lettuce-lined plates or 1 large lettuce-lined bowl. Sprinkle evenly with diced green pepper and serve.
Makes 4 servings.

CHINESE VERMICELLI WITH STIR-FRIED SHRIMP

Here is another recipe that makes use of quick and easy Chinese vermicelli.

4–5 ounces thin Chinese vermicelli
6 tablespoons peanut or vegetable oil
1 clove garlic, crushed
1 pound medium-size shrimp, shelled and deveined

1 tablespoon minced fresh ginger
1 tablespoon soy sauce
2 tablespoons fresh lemon juice
¼ cup minced scallions

Place vermicelli in a large, heat-proof bowl and pour over them sufficient boiling water to cover by about 2 inches. Let stand 3–4 minutes, then lift and separate strands with a fork. Let stand 3–4 minutes more or until tender. Drain into colander, blot dry, then transfer to a large bowl. Toss with 1 tablespoon of oil and set aside.

Pour 2 tablespoons of oil into a large, heavy skillet or wok over low heat. Add garlic and stir until limp but not browned. Remove and discard garlic. Raise heat to high. When oil is hot, add shrimp and minced ginger. Stir-fry until shrimp are firm and just lightly pink, about 2–3 minutes. Remove skillet from heat and stir in soy sauce, lemon juice, and remaining oil. Add shrimp mixture to vermicelli and toss to mix ingredients thoroughly. Sprinkle with scallions. Serve at room temperature.

If desired, serve with Marinated Mushrooms (see page 161).
Makes 4 servings.

SHELLS WITH SUN-DRIED TOMATOES

The intense flavor of the sun-dried tomatoes makes this an exceptional salad that is exceptionally easy to prepare.

5–6 ounces bottled sun-dried to-
    mato halves in olive oil,
    drained well and oil reserved
½ cup oil from sun-dried toma-
    toes
2 tablespoons balsamic or simi-
    lar vinegar
    Sprinkling of coarsely ground
    black pepper
8 ounces pasta shells
2 stalks celery, trimmed and
    thinly sliced at a 45-degree
    angle

1 small green pepper, seeded
    and cut into narrow strips
2–3 tablespoons mayonnaise, pref-
    erably homemade (see page
    181)
1–2 tablespoons fresh lemon juice
    Salt to taste
    Crisp lettuce leaves

Cut tomatoes into narrow strips and set aside.

Pour oil from jar of tomatoes into a large bowl and add vinegar and pepper. Set aside.

Cook pasta following directions on page 26. Drain into colander, then transfer to a bowl. Pour oil-vinegar mixture over pasta and toss lightly to mix. Add tomato strips. Let stand, tossing pasta occasionally until cooled to room temperature. Add celery and green pepper.

In a small bowl, combine mayonnaise with lemon juice. Add to salad mixture and toss again. Add salt to taste, keeping in mind that the tomatoes are already quite salty. If desired, refrigerate until about 30 minutes before serving.

Spoon salad into lettuce-lined bowl or onto individual salad plates.

Makes 4 servings.

Pasta salad with tahini dressing

An inspired mix of Italian and Mideastern cuisines.

2 tablespoons tahini paste
(available in gourmet shops)
1 8-ounce carton (1 cup) plain
yogurt
1-2 tablespoons pineapple juice,
apple juice, or fresh orange
juice
2 tablespoons minced fresh
parsley
1 cup shredded iceberg lettuce

2 tablespoons minced chives
Salt to taste
Freshly ground black pepper
to taste
8 ounces small pasta shapes
(shells, twists, corkscrews,
etc.)
4 ounces crumbled feta cheese
(optional)

To prepare dressing: In a large bowl, combine tahini paste and yogurt. Beat until smooth. Add pineapple juice and stir in parsley, lettuce, and chives. Season to taste with salt and pepper. Set aside at room temperature.

Cook pasta following directions on page 26. Drain into colander, then add to dressing mixture while still warm. Add cheese, if desired. Toss to mix. Serve at room temperature.
Makes 4–6 servings.

Second generation pasta salad

An Italian-American favorite. You'll love it!

1 tablespoon sherry wine vinegar
¼ cup olive oil
1 large clove garlic
½ teaspoon salt
8 ounces small pasta shells
1 7-ounce can tuna, drained and
flaked

1 large green pepper, cut into julienne strips
1 small mild red pepper or 2
green peppers, cut into julienne strips
2 tablespoons capers
6–8 Niçoise olives, chopped
Italian-style rolls

Place vinegar and oil into the bowl of a food processor or blender. Add garlic and salt. Process or blend briefly, only until garlic is finely minced. Pour into a large bowl.

Cook pasta following directions on page 26. Drain, then add to bowl with vinegar-oil mixture. Add tuna, peppers, and capers. Toss with 2 forks to mix. If desired, cover and refrigerate until 30 minutes before serving. Transfer to salad bowl. Sprinkle with chopped olives.

If desired, serve with crusty Italian-style rolls.

Makes 6–8 servings.

PASTA SALAD WITH VITELLO TONNATO

This Italian tuna and anchovy sauce can be made ahead and is often served over sliced cold roast veal. It is even better when tossed with pasta and served as a salad.

1 8-ounce can imported tuna
  packed in olive oil
3–4 anchovy filets, rinsed under
  cold running water and blotted thoroughly dry
1 tablespoon Dijon mustard
1 tablespoon lemon juice
¼ cup mild virgin olive oil
½ cup mayonnaise, preferably
  homemade (see page 181)

Coarsely ground black pepper
8 ounces small pasta shapes
4 stalks celery, trimmed, sliced
  into ½-inch lengths, and cut
  into narrow strips
¼ cup capers, drained
  Halved cherry tomatoes for
  garnish

In a medium bowl, combine undrained tuna with anchovies and mash with a fork to a chunky paste. Stir in mustard and lemon juice. Add oil, mayonnaise, and pepper to taste. Beat with a fork until smooth. Set aside.

Cook pasta following directions on page 26. Drain into colander and transfer to a large bowl. Add tuna mixture, celery, and capers, and toss to mix. If desired, cover salad and refrigerate several hours or until

ready to use, up to 24 hours. Transfer to a serving bowl and, if desired, garnish with cherry tomatoes.
Makes 4–6 servings.

MACARONI WITH ZUCCHINI

Here is proof positive that a great salad can be made with simple and inexpensive ingredients. The vegetables can be prepared ahead, and all that remains is to cook the pasta and combine with the remaining ingredients.

3 tablespoons peanut or vegetable oil
1 small clove garlic, crushed
½ teaspoon sugar
1 tablespoon apple cider vinegar
Salt
¼ teaspoon coarsely ground black pepper
1 large or 2 small zucchini, trimmed and diced

1 small green pepper, seeded, cored, and diced
1 small red or white onion, chopped
8 ounces small macaroni
1 tablespoon mayonnaise, preferably homemade (see page 181)
½ teaspoon bottled horseradish
Crisp lettuce leaves

At least one hour before serving, pour oil into a large, heavy skillet over low heat. Add garlic and cook, stirring, until very limp but not browned. Remove and discard garlic. Stir in sugar; when dissolved, pour into a large mixing bowl. Add vinegar, ½ teaspoon of salt, and pepper. Whisk until blended. Add zucchini, pepper, and onion. Let stand at room temperature about 1 hour or refrigerate several hours or overnight. Bring to room temperature before using

Cook macaroni following directions on page 26. Drain, then add to vegetable mixture. Add mayonnaise and horseradish and toss to mix ingredients thoroughly. Add additional salt to taste. If desired, refrigerate salad until 30 minutes before serving. Spoon onto lettuce-lined plates or into a large salad bowl.
Makes 6–8 servings.

FEDELINI WITH ZUCCHINI AND YELLOW SQUASH

This is our favorite salad in the late fall when fresh zucchini and squash can still be found in our market.

3 medium zucchini
3 medium yellow squash
  Salt
¼ cup olive oil
1 clove garlic, minced
2 tablespoons red wine vinegar
8 ounces fedelini
  Coarsely ground pepper to taste
1 teaspoon red pepper flakes
½ cup chopped black olives

Cut zucchini in ¼-inch slices; cut slices into narrow strips. Trim and cut squash into thin rounds. Place zucchini and squash into colander and sprinkle with 1 teaspoon of salt. Toss to coat. Let stand about 30 minutes to draw out the moisture. Wipe dry with paper toweling. Arrange slices and rounds in a single layer on a baking sheet and drizzle with oil. Place about 2 inches from broiler heat. Broil, turning once, until limp and lightly flecked with brown. Transfer to a large bowl and sprinkle with garlic. Stir in vinegar.

Cook fedelini following directions on page 26. Drain into colander. Add to vegetable mixture. Season lightly with salt and pepper. Stir in pepper flakes and olives. Serve at room temperature.

Makes 4 servings.

PASTA CAPONATA

This Sicilian specialty is often served as part of an antipasto platter with chunks of crusty Italian bread. Tossed with pasta, it becomes a superb salad, one you won't soon forget.

1 small (about 1 pound) eggplant
  Salt
2 large tomatoes
2 tablespoons peanut or vegetable
  oil
1 small onion, chopped
3 large stalks celery, chopped

¼ cup chopped pitted black olives
1 tablespoon pine nuts
2 teaspoons sugar
2 tablespoons red wine vinegar
¼ teaspoon coarsely ground black
  pepper
8 ounces small pasta shapes

Peel eggplant and cut into ½-inch cubes. Place into colander and sprinkle with ½ teaspoon of salt. Let stand at room temperature for about 30 minutes. Rinse cubes under cold water, tossing them to drain off excess salt. Blot dry with paper toweling. Place cubes in a large steamer pot over simmering water, cover, and let steam until tender, about 10 minutes. Transfer cubes to a large bowl. Set aside.

With a long-handled fork, plunge tomatoes one at a time into boiling water for about 30 seconds, then hold under cold running water and peel off skin. Cut in half and gently squeeze out seeds. Cut halves into thin strips and blot thoroughly dry with paper toweling. Set aside.

Pour oil into a large, heavy skillet over medium heat; when hot, add onion and celery. Sauté until crisp-tender. Add eggplant cubes, tomato strips, olives, and pine nuts. Cook, stirring, about 5 minutes. Sprinkle with sugar and stir until dissolved. Stir in vinegar and pepper. Scrape mixture into a large bowl and let stand until cooled to room temperature. If desired, refrigerate until about 30 minutes before using.

Cook pasta following directions on page 26. Drain into colander and add to caponata mixture. Toss to mix. Taste and add salt, if desired.
Makes 6–8 servings.

ZITI SALAD WITH ARTICHOKE HEARTS

Great picnic fare!

Mustard Vinaigrette (see
below)
12 ounces ziti
1 six-ounce jar marinated artichoke hearts, drained, chopped,
and marinade reserved
½ cup chopped red or green bell
pepper

½ cup bite-size cubes mozzarella
cheese
2 ounces Genoa salami, cut into
thin strips
¼ cup sliced pitted black olives

MUSTARD VINAIGRETTE

Reserved marinade from artichoke hearts plus sufficient
mild, fruity olive oil to measure
½ cup
1 tablespoon white wine vinegar

½ teaspoon sugar
½ teaspoon dry mustard
¼ teaspoon dried oregano
¼ teaspoon dried basil
Salt to taste

Prepare Mustard Vinaigrette. Pour measured marinade and oil from
artichokes into medium bowl. Add vinegar, sugar, mustard, oregano,
and basil. Beat with a fork until well mixed. Season to taste with salt.
Set aside until ready to use.

Cook ziti following directions on page 26. Drain into colander, then
transfer to a large bowl. Add artichokes, pepper, cheese, salami, and
olives. Pour dressing over surface of salad and mix with 2 forks to
combine ingredients thoroughly.

Makes 6-8 servings.

MEZZANI WITH SALMON AND BROCCOLI

This salad is extremely easy to prepare. It is light but filling, colorful and delicious.

1 10-ounce package frozen
  chopped broccoli
1 1-pound can salmon
2 tablespoons chopped fresh
  basil, or 2 teaspoons dried basil
1 teaspoon dried oregano
1 small purple onion, chopped
6 tablespoons mild olive oil, preferably extra-virgin

2 tablespoons red wine vinegar
  Salt to taste
  Coarsely ground black pepper
  to taste
8 ounces mezzani
1 large tomato, peeled, seeded,
  and chopped, and 2 tablespoons
  minced parsley for garnish (optional)

Cook frozen broccoli following package directions. Drain into colander, then transfer to a large bowl. Drain salmon, and break with a fork into large chunks, then add to broccoli. Add basil, oregano, onion, oil, and vinegar. Season lightly with salt and pepper. Set aside.

Cook mezzani following directions on page 26. Drain into colander, then add to salad mixture. Toss to mix thoroughly. Correct seasoning with additional salt and pepper.

Transfer salad to a larger serving bowl. If desired, garnish with chopped tomatoes and minced parsley.

Makes 6 servings.

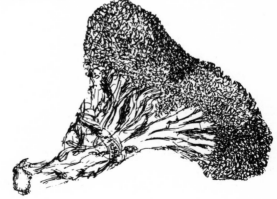

SPINACH FETTUCCINE SALAD WITH HAM AND BLUE CHEESE DRESSING

Festive, colorful, and filling!

Blue Cheese Dressing (see below)
8 ounces spinach fettuccine
6 ounces large mushrooms, trimmed and thinly sliced
4 ounces baked Virginia ham, thinly sliced and cut into narrow strips

½ cup minced parsley
½ cup chopped pitted black olives
½ cup thinly sliced celery

BLUE CHEESE DRESSING
1 cup sour cream or plain yogurt
1 tablespoon white wine vinegar
2 tablespoons crumbled blue cheese

Salt and pepper to taste

To prepare Blue Cheese Dressing: In a medium bowl, combine sour cream and vinegar and blend thoroughly. Fold in blue cheese. Add salt and pepper to taste. Set aside.

Cook fettuccine following directions on page 26. Drain into colander and transfer to a large bowl. Add Blue Cheese Dressing, mushrooms, ham, parsley, olives, and celery. Toss to mix.

Makes 6 servings.

SZECHUAN-STYLE SALAD WITH CHINESE VERMICELLI AND CHINESE CABBAGE

Here's a great salad to add to an Oriental-style buffet supper. No cooking is required—super easy to prepare.

¼ cup peanut or vegetable oil
2 tablespoons Oriental sesame oil
2 tablespoons soy sauce
2 tablespoons rice wine or white wine vinegar
1-2 teaspoons hot chili-flavored sesame oil
½ teaspoon salt or to taste

¼ teaspoon coarsely ground black pepper or to taste
1 large clove garlic, crushed
½ small head Chinese cabbage, cut lengthwise into long, thin julienne strips
½ cup mung bean sprouts
6-8 radishes, chopped
4-5 ounces thin Chinese vermicelli

At least 1 hour before serving, combine the peanut and Oriental sesame oils, soy sauce, vinegar, and hot chili-flavored sesame oil in a medium bowl. Beat with a fork until blended and smooth. Season with salt and pepper to taste. Add garlic. Let stand at room temperature for about 1 hour, or cover and refrigerate for several hours. Bring to room temperature before using. Remove and discard garlic. Set dressing aside.

In a large heat-proof bowl, place cabbage, bean sprouts, and radishes. Add boiling water to cover. Loose hulls from bean sprouts will float to the top. Gently pour off top water with loose hulls. Pour remaining water and vegetables into large colander; blot dry with paper toweling and transfer to a large salad bowl. Set aside. Place vermicelli in the same heat-proof bowl. Cover by about 2 inches with more boiling water. Let stand 4–5 minutes, then lift and separate strands with a fork. Let stand 3–4 minutes more or until tender. Pour into large colander. Blot vermicelli dry and add to vegetable mixture. Add dressing and toss to mix ingredients thoroughly. Serve at room temperature.

If desired, serve with rice crackers.

Makes 6–8 servings.

TORTELLINI SALAD

This inspired idea is so easy because half the work has already been done for you. The tortellini have already been deliciously stuffed. Just cook, add the vegetables, season nicely, and serve.

8 ounces cheese-stuffed freshly made or frozen tortellini
½ cup chopped celery
1 small green pepper, seeded and chopped
1 small Vidalia or other mild onion, chopped

½ cup chopped Niçoise olives
3 heaping tablespoons commercially prepared mayonnaise
1 tablespoon fresh lemon juice
2-3 dashes of Tabasco sauce
1 cup shredded romaine lettuce

Cook tortellini following package directions until *al dente*, about 6–8 minutes, or until tender. Drain into colander, then transfer to a mixing bowl. Add celery, green pepper, onion, and olives. Toss to mix.

In a small bowl, combine mayonnaise, lemon juice, and Tabasco sauce. Pour over tortellini mixture. Toss lightly. If desired, cover and refrigerate until 30 minutes before serving. Mix in lettuce and transfer to a serving bowl.

Makes 4–6 servings.

TORTELLINI WITH UNCOOKED TOMATO SAUCE

This hearty main-course pasta salad is filled with satisfying flavors. Served with thick slices of Italian-style bread and a light red wine, it makes an elegant meal. The vegetables can be prepared several hours or a day ahead. Complete the salad just before serving.

4 large tomatoes
1 large red bell pepper
2 cloves garlic, crushed
¼ cup minced parsley
¼ cup mild, fruity olive oil
2 tablespoons white or tarragon vinegar
½ teaspoon sugar
Coarse salt
Coarsely ground black pepper
12 ounces cheese- or meat-stuffed tortellini
½ cup pitted calabrese or cracked green olives

Several hours before serving: Using a long-handled fork, spear and plunge tomatoes 1 at a time into a large pot of boiling water for about 30 seconds. Hold under cold running water and slip off skin. Hold over a large mixing bowl and cut into bite-size chunks. Cut pepper into quarters, remove all seeds and white ribs, and cut into narrow strips. Add to bowl with tomatoes. Add garlic and stir in parsley. Add oil, vinegar, and sugar. Season lightly with salt and pepper. Stir to mix. To develop flavors, cover and refrigerate for several hours or overnight. Remove from refrigerator about 30 minutes before using. Remove and discard garlic.

Cook tortellini following package directions. Add to tomato mixture. Stir in olives. Serve at room temperature.

Makes 6 servings.

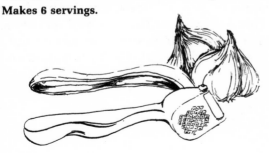

TRICOLOR ROTELLE SALAD

You'll find tricolor rotelle (made with egg, tomato, and spinach) at pasta shops and gourmet food shops across the country. Cooked *al dente*, tossed with black olive slices and cherry tomatoes, it makes an extremely colorful as well as flavorful salad.

Thin Mayonnaise Dressing (see below)
8 ounces tricolor rotelle
1 tablespoon mild olive oil, preferably extra-virgin
½ cup sliced pitted black and green olives

¼ cup chopped fresh parsley
2 tablespoons chopped fresh basil leaves
½ cup chopped fresh chives
Salt to taste
4 cherry tomatoes and parsley sprigs for garnish

THIN MAYONNAISE DRESSING
1 egg yolk
1 tablespoon white wine vinegar
½ teaspoon Dijon mustard
½ teaspoon salt or to taste

Coarsely ground black pepper to taste
3 tablespoons peanut or vegetable oil

To prepare Thin Mayonnaise Dressing: Place egg yolk in a medium bowl and beat with fork until light and lemony. Beat in vinegar and mustard. Season to taste with salt and pepper. Slowly add oil, beating as added. Continue to beat until mixture is thickened. (Or: Place egg yolk, vinegar, and mustard in the bowl of a food processor. Process until blended. With motor running, slowly add oil in a thin, steady stream. Continue to process until mixture thickens slightly.) Set aside at room temperature.

Cook pasta following directions on page 26. Drain, transfer to a large bowl, and toss to mix. Add Thin Mayonnaise Dressing and remaining ingredients and toss to mix thoroughly. If desired, refrigerate until about 1 hour before serving. Garnish with whole cherry tomatoes and parsley sprigs.

Makes 4–6 servings.

Rigatoni Salad with Fresh Tomato and Zucchini Sauce

This classic Italian salad can be made ahead. It is just perfect for lazy summer days. Serve with crostini (crusty Italian bread) and a fruity white wine.

2 small, firm zucchini
3 large or 4 small sun-ripened tomatoes
1 small Vidalia onion, peeled and chopped
8–12 fresh basil leaves, torn into small pieces, or 2 teaspoons dried basil leaves, crumbled
½ cup fruity olive oil
1 tablespoon tarragon or white wine vinegar
1 teaspoon coarse salt or to taste
Coarsely ground black pepper to taste

4 ounces coarsely grated mozzarella cheese
12 ounces rigatoni

At least 2 hours before serving, trim and shred zucchini, using the coarse side of a hand grater or a food processor with shredding attachment. Place shreds in a clean dish towel, bring ends together, and twist towel, squeezing the shreds dry. Place in a large mixing bowl. With a long-handled fork, plunge tomatoes 1 at a time in a large pan of rapidly boiling water for about 30 seconds; rinse under cold water and peel off skin. Hold over bowl with zucchini and cut into small chunks, letting chunks fall into bowl. Add onion, basil, olive oil, and vinegar. Toss to mix, then season with salt and pepper to taste. Let stand at room temperature for about 2 hours or cover and refrigerate for several hours, but bring to room temperature before using. Add cheese and toss to mix.

Cook pasta following directions on page 26. Drain into colander, then add while hot to tomato mixture. Serve at room temperature.
Makes 4 servings.

GARDEN PASTA SALAD

For a quick and easy menu, serve this salad with assorted finger sandwiches and a pleasurable, fruity white wine.

1 cup mayonnaise, homemade
(see page 181) or store-bought
¼ cup minced parsley
3 tablespoons chopped fresh basil
leaves, or 1 teaspoon crushed
dried basil
4 ounces sharp cheddar cheese,
crumbled

1 cup thinly sliced celery
¼ cup trimmed and thinly sliced
radishes
½ cup chopped walnuts
8 ounces corkscrew noodles
2 medium sun-ripened tomatoes,
cut into wedges

In a large bowl, combine mayonnaise, parsley, and basil. Stir in cheese, celery, radishes, and walnuts.

Cook noodles following directions on page 26. Drain into colander, then add to mayonnaise-vegetable mixture.

Spoon salad into a large, decorative bowl and surround edges of bowl with tomato wedges.

Makes 4–6 servings.

Seashell salad

We like to serve this salad with pita bread triangles and ice-cold beer.

1 tablespoon peanut or vegetable oil
½ teaspoon Oriental sesame oil
1 medium zucchini, trimmed and coarsely chopped
2 small yellow squash, trimmed and coarsely chopped
1 pound medium shrimp, peeled and deveined
8 ounces maruzze (seashell-shaped pasta)

1 cup thick mayonnaise, homemade (see page 181) or store-bought
1 tablespoon mustard
Salt and pepper to taste
6–8 cracked green olives, pitted and cut into thin slivers
Garlicky Pita Bread Triangles (see page 169)

Pour peanut and sesame oils into a large, heavy skillet or wok over medium heat. When hot, add zucchini, yellow squash, and shrimp. Stir-fry until shrimp are firm and pink, and vegetables crisp-tender, about 3 minutes. Transfer mixture to a large bowl. Set aside.

Cook pasta following directions on page 26. Drain into colander, then add to vegetable mixture.

In a small bowl, combine mayonnaise, mustard, salt, and pepper. Add to pasta-vegetable mixture. Add olives. Toss gently but thoroughly. If desired, cover salad and refrigerate until about 30 minutes before serving. Transfer salad to a large, decorative bowl; if desired, surround edges of bowl with Garlicky Pita Bread Triangles.

Makes 6–8 servings.

TASTY SALADS MADE FROM RICE AND OTHER GRAINS

3.

Rice salads are wonderfully light yet filling, extremely nutritious yet low-calorie. Best of all they look positively beautiful.

The success of a rice salad depends both on the type of rice and the way it is cooked. You need fluffy, well-drained rice with each kernel separate. And the rice should have distinctive flavor. Although many rices measure up to one or the other of these requirements, those that meet both, and are thus best suited for salads, are long-grained Carolina white rice, imported Italian Arborio rice, and basmati rice from India. These rices have an added attraction: They can be prepared ahead and stored in the refrigerator until you are ready to combine them with other ingredients.

COOKING RICE

To cook long-grain Carolina rice, imported Italian Arborio rice, or basmati rice, pour about 6 cups of cold water into a large saucepan and bring to a full boil over high heat. Add about 1 teaspoon of peanut or vegetable oil and ½ teaspoon of salt. Slowly add 1–1½ cups of rice so that the water continues to simmer. Return water to a full boil and stir rice with a long-handled fork or spoon to keep it from sticking to the bottom of the pan. Lower heat slightly and let rice cook, uncovered, at a brisk simmer, stirring occasionally until just tender, about 15–20 minutes. Drain into colander, transfer to a large bowl, and immediately stir in about 1 tablespoon of peanut or vegetable oil. Let "cook" slightly, then toss with 2 forks to mix. If desired, cover bowl with plastic wrap and refrigerate rice for up to 48 hours, or until you are ready to prepare the salad.

One cup of rice will yield about 3 cups of cooked rice.

To cook wild rice for salads, pour about 6 cups of cold water into a large saucepan and bring to a full boil over high heat. Slowly add rice so that water continues to simmer. Return water to a full boil and allow to boil for 2–3 minutes, or until water is covered with a thin layer of grayish-white foam. Remove pot from heat and let stand until boiling subsides and rice has settled to the bottom of the pot. Gently pour off top foam and almost all of the water. Add about 5½ cups of cold fresh water, return pot to heat, and again bring to a boil. If additional foam appears on top of the water, again remove the pot from the heat, let rice settle to the bottom of the pot, and pour off foam and about 1 cup of water. Replace with fresh cold water and return pot to heat. Let this water come to a full boil, then lower heat and add about 1 teaspoon of peanut or vegetable oil and ½ teaspoon of salt. Let rice cook at a brisk simmer until tender, adding additional cold water as needed to keep rice covered by about 1 inch. It will take 25–35 minutes for rice to cook, depending on the variety of wild rice used.

One cup of wild rice will yield about 3 cups of cooked rice.

Basque salad

Here is a hearty saffron rice salad with salami, pepperoni, and baked Virginia ham.

1 8-ounce package frozen, peeled, and deveined cooked "popcorn" tiny shrimp
2 tablespoons dry sherry wine
2 tablespoons peanut or vegetable oil
1 small white onion, chopped
1 teaspoon whole saffron
2½ cups water
1 cup imported Italian Arborio rice
4 ounces each: hard salami and pepperoni, cut into julienne strips

4 ounces baked Virginia ham, cut into julienne strips
½ small green pepper cut into strips
1 2–2½-ounce jar chopped pimientos, drained
Salt to taste
Coarsely ground black pepper to taste
¼ cup minced parsley

Place shrimp into colander and let stand until thawed. Transfer to a small bowl and add sherry. Cover and refrigerate until ready to use.

Pour oil into a large, heavy skillet over low heat. Add onion and cook, stirring, until limp. Stir in saffron. Raise heat to high and add water. Bring to a full boil, then slowly add rice so that water continues to boil. Lower heat, cover pot, and let rice simmer for about 20 minutes or until tender and almost all water has been absorbed. Remove from heat and let stand for about 5 minutes. Drain into colander, then transfer to a large bowl and fluff with 2 forks to separate grains. Add salami, pepperoni, ham, green pepper, and chopped pimientos. Drain shrimp and add to bowl. Season to taste with salt and pepper. Toss thoroughly. Arrange on a large platter, sprinkle surface with parsley, and serve at room temperature.

Makes 6–8 servings.

CHICKEN AND RICE SALAD

This makes a wonderfully flavorful departure from the usual chicken salad.

1 cup basmati, Italian Arborio, or long-grain Carolina rice
2 cups diced cooked chicken
6 ounces marinated artichoke hearts
½ cup chopped green onion
Minced parsley

1–2 tablespoons red wine vinegar, or to taste
Fruity olive oil to taste
Salt to taste
Coarsely ground black pepper to taste
Crisp lettuce leaves

Cook rice following directions on page 84. Drain into colander and transfer to a large bowl. Add chicken. Chop artichoke hearts coarsely and add to rice-chicken mixture. Add green onion and ¼ cup of parsley. Toss lightly.

Pour marinade from artichokes into a small bowl. Add vinegar and oil. Whisk until blended. Season to taste with salt and pepper. Pour over rice mixture and toss to combine ingredients thoroughly. Transfer to a lettuce-lined bowl. Garnish, if desired, with additional minced parsley.

If desired, serve with Parsley Butter Fingers (see page 165).

Makes 4–6 servings.

CRAB AND RICE SALAD IN AVOCADO SHELLS

This is pure elegance. But aren't avocados high in calories and isn't crab meat expensive? The answer to both questions is yes and no. Because the crab meat is mixed with other ingredients, a small amount will go a long way. As for the avocados, they are not only loaded with good-for-you nutrients but are also lower in calories than a small portion of meat. Eat and enjoy.

1 tablespoon best-quality extra-virgin olive oil
2 teaspoons sherry wine vinegar
½ teaspoon salt
¼ teaspoon pepper
½ cup imported Italian Arborio rice
1 stalk celery, minced
1 small zucchini, trimmed and minced

8 ounces fresh or frozen lump crab meat, thawed
2 large ripe avocados
Juice of 1 small lemon
4 large, slightly rounded lettuce leaves
2–3 tablespoons thick mayonnaise, homemade (see page 181) or store-bought (optional)
Paprika

In a small bowl, combine oil, vinegar, salt, and pepper. Beat with a fork to mix. Set aside. Cook rice following directions on page 84. Drain as directed, then immediately transfer to a large bowl. Add the oil-vinegar mixture while the rice is still hot and toss with 2 forks to mix. Add celery, zucchini, and crab meat. Toss again with forks to incorporate ingredients. If desired, refrigerate until ready to serve.

Cut each avocado in half, then remove and discard stones. Peel each half and brush with lemon juice. Place each half on a lettuce-lined salad plate and spoon one-fourth of crab meat mixture over each, letting excess fall onto lettuce. If desired, top each with a dollop of mayonnaise. Sprinkle with paprika. Serve at once.

Makes 4 servings.

FRUITED RICE SALAD

Though I find most fruit salads rather trite and dull, this one makes an especially pleasurable addition to a midsummer luncheon buffet.

1 cup basmati, Italian Arborio, or
    long-grain Carolina rice
    Peanut or vegetable oil
2 tablespoons sugar
    Pinch of dry mustard
½ teaspoon salt
2 tablespoons white wine vinegar
1 tablespoon minced green onion

2 teaspoons poppy seeds
1 large navel orange, peeled and
    sectioned
1 8-ounce can pineapple sections,
    drained
½ cup sliced strawberries
    Whole strawberries and pecan
    halves for garnish (optional)

Cook rice following directions on page 84. Drain into colander and transfer while still warm to a large bowl. Add 1 tablespoon of oil and toss lightly to mix. Set aside at room temperature until cool.

In a bowl, combine sugar, mustard, salt, and vinegar. Beat with fork or hand mixer until sugar has dissolved, or place in blender or food processor and process until sugar has dissolved. Gradually beat or blend in ½ cup of oil. When mixture thickens, add green onion and poppy seeds. Pour over rice. Add orange and pineapple sections and sliced strawberries. Toss lightly to mix ingredients. Transfer to a serving bowl and garnish, if desired, with whole strawberries and pecan halves.

Makes 6–8 servings.

INDONESIAN-STYLE RICE SALAD WITH SHRIMP

This colorful salad is as good to eat as it is beautiful to see.

1 cup imported basmati rice
Peanut or vegetable oil
1 clove garlic, crushed
1 1-inch cube fresh ginger root,
   peeled and crushed
1 pound medium shrimp, peeled,
   deveined, and coarsely chopped
½ cup frozen green peas, thawed

1 cup mung bean sprouts, rinsed
   and blotted dry
½ teaspoon Oriental sesame oil
1 tablespoon soy sauce
1 tablespoon Oriental rice wine
   vinegar
1 cup dry-roasted peanuts

Cook rice following directions on page 84. Drain into colander, then transfer to a large bowl. Set aside.

Pour 1 tablespoon of peanut oil into a large, heavy skillet or wok over low heat. Add garlic and ginger. Cook, stirring frequently, until garlic is limp. Remove and discard garlic and ginger. Add shrimp and stir-fry until firm and pink, about 2 minutes. Stir in peas and cook, stirring, for about 1 minute. Stir in bean sprouts. Remove skillet or wok from heat. Stir in sesame oil, soy sauce, 1 teaspoon of peanut oil, and vinegar. Scrape mixture over rice. Add peanuts. Toss to mix thoroughly. Serve at room temperature.

Makes 4–6 servings.

LETTUCE LEAF DOLMATHIS

Serve this Near Eastern-style salad as the first course of a seated dinner party featuring roast leg of lamb or with cold sliced leg of lamb as part of a buffet supper.

Peanut or vegetable oil
1 teaspoon salt
½ cup long-grain white rice
1 medium-size white or purple onion, minced
¼ cup raisins
1 tablespoon sugar
¼ teaspoon coarsely ground black pepper
¼ cup chopped pimiento-stuffed olives

1 tablespoon fresh lemon juice
20–24 large thick leaves of iceberg lettuce
2–3 dashes of Tabasco sauce (optional)
1½ cups chicken stock or broth, homemade or store-bought

In a large saucepan, bring 1½ cups of water to a full boil. Stir in ½ teaspoon of oil and ½ teaspoon of salt. Add rice and simmer for 8–10 minutes or until rice is partially cooked. Drain into colander, then transfer to a large bowl. Set aside.

Pour 3 tablespoons of oil into a large, heavy skillet over medium heat. Add onion and stir until transparent. Stir in raisins, sugar, remaining salt, and pepper. Stir until sugar has dissolved. Remove skillet from heat and stir in olives and lemon juice. Scrape mixture over rice in bowl. Set aside.

Preheat oven to 350 degrees Fahrenheit. Bring a large pot of water to a full boil. Spear lettuce leaves one at a time with the tines of a long-handled fork and hold in boiling water until limp. Spread out on flat surface and blot thoroughly dry with paper toweling. Spoon ½–1½ teaspoons of rice mixture in center of leaf. Fold sides of leaf over filling, then roll up loosely, allowing some room for the rice to expand as it cooks. Place rolls, as prepared, seam side down in a long, shallow (2 inches by 6 inches by 9 inches) glass baking dish. Stir Tabasco sauce into chicken stock and pour over rolls. Cover dish loosely with foil and bake for 30 minutes. Remove dish from oven and cool rolls in broth to room temperature. If desired, refrigerate until ready to serve. Pour off and discard any broth that has not been absorbed. Serve dolmathis on individual salad plates or on a long platter.

If desired, serve with Sliced Tomatoes Sicilian-Style and Onion Rolls (see pages 160 and 170).

Makes 20–24 dolmathis.

NUTTY RICE SALAD WITH LETTUCE AND OLD-FASHIONED FRENCH DRESSING

Serve with baked Virginia ham and pickled peaches for a southern-style back-porch supper.

Southern French Dressing (see below)
1 cup long-grain white rice
1 cup chopped walnuts or pecans
½ cup raisins

1 small tart apple, peeled, seeded, and chopped
1 cup shredded romaine or iceberg lettuce
¼ cup minced green onion

SOUTHERN FRENCH DRESSING
1 egg
¼ cup apple cider vinegar
1 tablespoon sugar

1 teaspoon Creole-style mustard
½ cup peanut or vegetable oil
½ teaspoon salt

To prepare Southern French Dressing: Combine egg, vinegar, sugar, and mustard in the bowl of a food processor or blender. Process or blend until sugar has dissolved and mixture is smooth. With machine running, slowly add oil in a steady stream. Transfer to a small bowl. Add salt to taste. If desired, cover and refrigerate until ready to use.

Cook rice following directions on page 84. Drain into colander, then transfer to a large bowl. Add walnuts, raisins, chopped apple, shredded lettuce, and green onion. Add dressing and toss lightly to mix.

Makes 4–6 servings.

NEAR EASTERN LENTIL AND BASMATI RICE SALAD

In this country, lentils were considered for a long time as only hearty winter fare. But they make delicious summer salads. You'll find both pink lentils and basmati rice in Near Eastern markets, health food stores, and gourmet food shops.

1 8-ounce package lentils
1 clove garlic, crushed
  Salt
2 tablespoons red wine vinegar
  Mild virgin olive oil
½ cup basmati rice (long-grain white rice can be substituted)
1 small Vidalia (purple) onion, chopped
½ cup very thinly sliced celery
½ cup coarsely chopped radishes
2 heaping tablespoons mango chutney (large pieces of chutney finely chopped)
  Pepper to taste

In a large pot, soak lentils for about 2 hours in cold water to cover. Drain, cover with fresh water, and bring to a boil over medium heat. Add garlic. Lower heat and let cook at a brisk simmer until tender but not mushy. Drain into colander and transfer to a bowl. Remove and discard garlic; add 1 teaspoon of salt, vinegar, and ¼ cup of oil.

Cook rice following directions on page 84. Drain into colander, then add to lentil mixture. Add remaining ingredients and additional salt to taste. Toss to mix. Cover and refrigerate salad until about 30 minutes before serving.

Makes 8 servings.

RICE SALAD WITH MANGO CHUTNEY MAYONNAISE

Rice and ham complement each other naturally; Mango Chutney Mayonnaise adds Near Eastern flavor.

Mango Chutney Mayonnaise
(see below)
1 cup long-grain white rice or
basmati rice
8 ounces finely diced baked ham
1 small green pepper, chopped

½ cup finely chopped celery
½ cup mung bean sprouts, rinsed
and blotted dry
Crisp lettuce leaves
Tomato wedges for garnish

MANGO CHUTNEY MAYONNAISE
½ cup mayonnaise
2 tablespoons fresh lemon juice

3 heaping tablespoons mango
chutney

To prepare Mango Chutney Mayonnaise: In a small bowl, combine all ingredients and stir until well blended. Set aside.

Cook rice following directions on page 84, then transfer to a large bowl. Add ham, green pepper, celery, and bean sprouts. Stir in Mango Chutney Mayonnaise. If desired, cover bowl and refrigerate salad until about 30 minutes before serving.

Line a decorative salad bowl or 6 salad plates with crisp lettuce leaves. Top with salad and garnish with tomato wedges.

Makes 6 servings.

RICE SALAD WITH APPLES AND RAISINS

We prepare this salad in early fall when we can find tart, crisp apples that have not been waxed for supermarket presentation.

1 tablespoon peanut or vegetable
  oil
1 small white onion, minced
1 cup long-grain white rice
1 cup unsweetened apple juice
1 cup water
2 tablespoons lemon juice
1 teaspoon salt
2 tablespoons mild olive oil

¼ cup raisins
2 teaspoons apple cider vinegar
2 medium-size unpeeled tart,
  crisp apples
2 green onions, trimmed and
  chopped
½ cup minced parsley
  Parsley sprigs for garnish (optional)

Pour peanut oil into a large saucepan over medium heat. Add onion and rice; stir until rice is transparent, about 2 minutes. Pour in apple juice, water, and lemon juice. Bring liquid to a full boil, stirring rice occasionally. Add salt. Lower heat, cover pot, and let rice simmer until almost all liquid has been absorbed. Drain into colander, then transfer to a large bowl. Cool to room temperature.

Pour olive oil into a small bowl and add raisins. Let stand for about 10 minutes or until raisins are plump. Add vinegar and stir to mix. Add to rice and toss with 2 forks to incorporate ingredients. If desired, refrigerate until about 30 minutes before serving.

Core each apple and remove seeds; do not peel. Cut each into small cubes and add to rice mixture. Using 2 forks, toss salad again to mix in apples. Transfer to a serving bowl. Sprinkle green onions and minced parsley over surface and, if desired, surround edge of bowl with parsley sprigs.

Makes 4–6 servings.

RICE AND VIRGINIA BAKED HAM SALAD

This salad puts together a marvelous combination of flavors that has a touch of the South.

¾ cup mayonnaise, preferably homemade (see page 181)
1 tablespoon lemon juice
1 tablespoon honey
1 cup cooked long-grain white rice
8 ounces cubed Virginia baked ham
1 cup frozen green peas, thawed

½ cup chopped black olives
¼ cup chopped green onion
2 tender celery stalks, diced
Salt and pepper to taste
4 large Boston lettuce leaves
4 small ripe tomatoes, cored and sliced from top to bottom
1 tablespoon minced parsley for garnish

In a medium bowl, combine mayonnaise, lemon juice, and honey. Set aside.

In a large bowl, combine rice, ham, peas, olives, onion, and celery. Fold in mayonnaise mixture and blend well. Add salt and pepper to taste.

Place lettuce leaves on salad plates and spread tomato slices in a fan arrangement. Top with rice-ham salad and garnish with minced parsley.

Makes 4 servings.

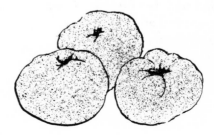

Roz cole's near eastern salad

An authentic recipe? No, of course not. The theme is Near Eastern, but the adaptation is much more flavorful. This is a typical example of how an American recipe develops.

1 cup raw basmati rice
1 teaspoon sesame oil
¼ teaspoon salt
¼ cup orange juice
2 tablespoons soy sauce
1 tablespoon honey
2 tablespoons rice wine vinegar
1 8-ounce can crushed pineapple, drained
2–3 green onions, trimmed and
   chopped
2–3 stalks celery, trimmed and
   chopped
½ cup mung bean sprouts
½ cup raisins

¼ cup chopped cashew nuts
1 small green pepper, chopped
1 small red pepper, chopped
6–8 fresh snow peas, trimmed and
   split in half lengthwise, for
   garnish (optional)

In a large saucepan, bring 3½ cups of water to a full boil. Slowly add rice so that water continues to boil. Stir in sesame oil and salt. Lower heat and let simmer until rice is tender. Drain into colander, then transfer while still hot to a large bowl. Add orange juice, soy sauce, honey, vinegar, and pineapple. Toss to mix. Let stand at room temperature about 15 minutes, then add green onion, celery, bean sprouts, raisins, and cashews. Toss lightly. If desired, refrigerate until about 30 minutes before serving. Transfer to a large serving bowl. Sprinkle top of salad with red and green peppers. If desired, arrange snow peas in a circle around edge of bowl.

Makes 6–8 servings.

TOMATOES STUFFED WITH TABBOULEH SALAD

Try this salad for splendid buffet party fare. It is colorful, different, delicious, and easy to serve.

¾ cup tabbouleh (cracked wheat)
¼ cup finely chopped scallions
¼ cup finely chopped parsley
¼ cup ripe pitted olives
¼ cup raisins
¼ cup chopped almonds
¼ cup fresh finely chopped mint leaves, or 2 tablespoons dried mint leaves

¼ cup olive or vegetable oil
¼ cup lemon juice
   Salt and pepper to taste
6 large ripe tomatoes
   Whole small romaine lettuce leaves
   Small ripe pitted olives for garnish (optional)

In a large bowl, cover tabbouleh with boiling water by about 2 inches, then let stand for about 1 hour at room temperature. Drain well and blot thoroughly dry with paper toweling. Fluff with a fork. Add the scallions, parsley, olives, raisins, almonds, and mint.

In a small bowl, combine the oil and lemon juice. Pour over salad mixture. Toss to mix, then season to taste with salt and pepper. Let stand in a cool place for about 1 hour, or cover and refrigerate until about 30 minutes before using.

Cut each tomato in half and gently squeeze out seeds and juice. Carefully scoop out pulp. Blot pulp dry, cut into small dice, and add to salad mixture. Sprinkle each tomato half lightly with salt and place upside down on paper towels to drain. Place each tomato half, cut side up, on lettuce-lined plate. Fill with tabbouleh mixture, mounding it high and letting excess fall onto lettuce. Garnish with olives, if desired. **Makes 6 servings.**

Walnut Tabbouleh

Bulgur was once considered just "health food," but mixed with chopped walnuts and fresh vegetables and tossed with a walnut oil vinaigrette, it becomes an exceptionally flavorful salad.

1 large or 2 medium tomatoes	2 tablespoons fresh lemon juice
¾ cup bulgur	Salt to taste
¼ cup finely minced parsley	Coarsely ground black pepper
½ cup finely chopped green onion	to taste
¼ cup finely chopped fresh mint	1 cup peeled, seeded, and cubed
½ cup chopped walnuts	cucumbers and fresh mint
2 tablespoons walnut oil	sprigs for garnish (optional)

Cut tomatoes in half and squeeze out all seeds and juice; cut halves into narrow strips. Set aside.

Place bulgur in a large bowl and add boiling water to cover by about 1 inch; let stand until all water has been absorbed. Spoon wheat onto a large, clean, dry dish towel; roll up and squeeze until very dry. Transfer to a second large bowl. Add tomato strips, parsley, green onion, mint, and walnuts. Toss to mix. Add oil and lemon juice. Toss again, then season to taste with salt and pepper. If desired, salad may be covered and refrigerated until about 30 minutes before serving. Garnish, if you wish, with cucumber cubes and fresh mint.

Makes 6–8 servings.

WILD AND WHITE RICE SALAD

This is a wonderfully flavorful salad and a great addition to a large buffet-style luncheon or supper party.

Red Wine Vinaigrette Dressing (see below)
½ cup raisins
2 tablespoons medium dry sherry
8 ounces mixed wild and white rice

1 large or 2 small tomatoes, peeled, seeded, and chopped
1 small Vidalia onion, peeled and minced
2–3 stalks celery, chopped
¼ cup minced parsley
¼ cup slivered almonds

RED WINE VINAIGRETTE DRESSING
¼ cup peanut or vegetable oil
1 tablespoon olive oil
2 tablespoons dry red wine vinegar
1 tablespoon Dijon or coarse ground Creole mustard

Salt to taste
Coarsely ground black pepper to taste

To prepare Red Wine Vinaigrette Dressing: In a small bowl, combine oils and vinegar and beat until blended. Stir in mustard. Season to taste with salt and pepper. Set aside until ready to use.

Place raisins and sherry in a small bowl, then set aside until ready to use.

Cook rice following directions on page 84. Drain into colander, then transfer to a large bowl. Add Vinaigrette Dressing and toss lightly to mix. Add tomatoes, onion, celery, parsley, and almonds. Add raisins and any sherry that has not been absorbed. Toss salad with 2 forks, blending thoroughly. If desired, cover and refrigerate until about 30 minutes before serving.

Makes 8–12 servings.

WILD RICE WALDORF SALAD

Here is a gourmet version of an old favorite, classic Waldorf salad. Great party fare!

4 ounces wild rice
2 tablespoons fresh or canned
  pineapple juice
3 slices fresh pineapple, cored
  and diced, or 1 8-ounce can
  pineapple tidbits in natural
  juice, drained
½ cup diced celery

2 medium-size tart, crisp apples,
  cored and chopped
2½ ounces (about ¾ cup) walnuts,
  chopped
¾ cup mayonnaise, preferably
  homemade (see page 181)
Crisp lettuce leaves

Cook wild rice following directions on page 84. Drain into colander, then transfer to a large bowl. Stir in pineapple juice. Add pineapple, celery, apples, walnuts, and mayonnaise. Toss thoroughly to combine ingredients. Refrigerate until chilled or until ready to serve. Spoon into lettuce-lined bowls. If desired, serve with Parsley Butter Fingers (see page 165).

Makes 8–10 servings.

WILD RICE AND GARDEN FRESH VEGETABLE SALAD

Serve this truly elegant salad as part of your next party buffet supper.

4 ounces wild rice
½ cup trimmed and chopped
  radishes
4 ounces mushrooms, cleaned,
  trimmed, and coarsely chopped
1 medium-size cucumber, peeled,
  seeded, and chopped

1 tablespoon coarsely chopped
  large capers
¼ cup minced parsley
  Cumin Dressing (see page 180)
  Crisp spinach leaves (optional)

Cook wild rice following directions on page 84. Drain into colander, then transfer to a large bowl. Add radishes, mushrooms, cucumber, capers, and parsley. Stir to combine ingredients. Add Cumin Dressing and toss to mix. Refrigerate until chilled or until ready to serve. Spoon into spinach-lined salad bowl. If desired, serve with Tomato Sandwich Rounds (see page 168).

Makes 8–10 servings.

GREAT POTATO SALADS

4.

To prepare a great potato salad, the only important thing you need to know is that you must start with freshly cooked, hot potatoes. Using cold, leftover potatoes can be justified only on economic grounds, never culinary ones. Stubborn and impenetrable, a cold potato resists any seasoning, however flavorful it may be. A salad made with cold potatoes is like reading yesterday's newspaper. On the other hand, a potato salad made with freshly cooked, still-hot potatoes that are low in starch and firm in texture is probably the most deliciously satisfying way to prepare the lowly potato.

For a truly memorable potato salad, all you need to do is boil, peel, then slice or dice the hot potatoes into a large bowl. Firm, waxy, new potatoes and small red potatoes are the preferred choices for salad making, though you may also use any so-called boiling potato you find in your market. Dress them while they are still hot with a simple Vinaigrette Dressing: 1 tablespoon of oil, 1 teaspoon of vinegar, and ½ teaspoon of salt for every 2½–3 pounds of potatoes. It will be quickly absorbed by the receptive potatoes and will flavor them all the way through to the center as they cool. You may then proceed with your recipe to complete the salad. Even when making your mother's favorite old-fashioned potato salad, you'll notice a tremendous improvement in flavor if the potatoes are prepared in this manner.

In this section you'll find potato salads ranging from updated old-fashioned American to classic French, as well as many other exciting variations on these themes.

CLASSIC FRENCH POTATO SALAD

This is perhaps the best potato salad of all.

½ cup light, fruity olive oil
¼ cup red or white wine vinegar
1 tablespoon Dijon or similar mustard

Salt
Freshly ground black pepper to taste

2½–3 pounds small new potatoes,
   all approximately the same
   size
½ cup finely peeled minced
   scallions

¼ cup minced parsley, preferably flat-leaf

In a small bowl, combine olive oil and vinegar; beat with a fork until blended. Stir in mustard and 2 teaspoons of salt. Add black pepper to taste. Set aside.

Bring a large pot of water to a full boil. Scrub potatoes and drop them into the boiling water. Cook at a brisk simmer until sufficiently tender to pierce with the point of a small knife. Drain into colander. Hold potatoes 1 at a time under cool running water and slip off skin. Slice immediately into ½-inch rounds, letting rounds fall into a large bowl.

Whisk the oil–vinegar mixture to reblend and pour over hot potatoes. Using a rubber spatula, toss potatoes gently to coat well. Add scallions and parsley. Toss gently again to mix. Taste and add additional salt if desired. Serve at room temperature.

If desired, serve with Cucumbers in Sour Cream (see page 157).

Makes 4–6 servings.

GARLICKY POTATO SALAD

Garlic lovers, this one's for you.

6 large cloves garlic, peeled
   and crushed
Salt
2½–3 pounds boiling potatoes
2 tablespoons Vinaigrette
   Dressing (see page 174)
½–1 cup mayonnaise, preferably
   homemade (see page 181)
1 large dill pickle, chopped
   (about ¾ cup)

½ cup thinly sliced radishes
   (optional)
½ cup chopped celery (op-
   tional)
½ cup chopped parsley (optional)
Coarsely ground black pepper to taste

In a large pot bring 3–4 quarts of water to a full boil; add garlic and 2 teaspoons of salt. Lower heat and let simmer about 30 minutes.

While water boils, peel potatoes and cut into bite-size chunks, letting chunks fall into a large bowl of cold water.

With a slotted spoon, remove and disgard garlic from water. Drain potatoes, add them to boiling water, and let cook until tender. Drain into colander, then shake colander to dry potatoes thoroughly. Transfer to a large bowl. Add Vinaigrette Dressing and toss lightly to mix. Let stand until potatoes have absorbed dressing. Fold in mayonnaise. Add pickles and, if desired, radishes, celery, and parsley. Season with salt and pepper to taste. Toss to mix ingredients thoroughly. Serve at room temperature.

Makes 4–6 servings.

OLD-FASHIONED AMERICAN POTATO SALAD

This one is great for Fourth of July picnics, family reunions, and such.

2½–3 pounds boiling potatoes
  2 tablespoons Vinaigrette Dressing (see page 174)
  4 hard-cooked eggs, peeled and chopped
4–6 green onions, trimmed and chopped
  3 stalks celery, trimmed and chopped

1 teaspoon celery seed
¼ cup minced parsley
2 tablespoons fresh lemon juice
1 cup mayonnaise, preferably homemade (see page 181)
Salt and pepper to taste

Place potatoes in a large, heavy pot. Add sufficient water to cover by about 1 inch. Place over medium heat and bring to a boil. Partially cover pot, lower heat, and let water simmer until potatoes are tender but not falling apart. Drain into colander. Hold potatoes 1 at a time under running water, and slip off skin. Chop into small cubes, letting cubes fall into a large bowl. Add Vinaigrette Dressing and toss lightly. Set aside until cool. Add hard-cooked eggs, green onions, celery, celery seed, and parsley. Toss to distribute ingredients.

In a small bowl, combine lemon juice and mayonnaise. Beat with a fork to blend. Pour over potato mixture and gently fold until all ingredients are coated. Add salt and pepper to taste. Set salad aside until ready to serve but do not refrigerate. Serve slightly warm or at room temperature.

Makes 6–8 servings.

HEARTY POTATO SALAD WITH BEEF

Meat and potatoes, a class partnership, make this salad a national favorite.

2½–3 small new potatoes
  ½ cup finely chopped green
    onion
  1 cup finely chopped celery
  4 ounces roast beef, chopped
  ¼ cup chopped sour pickle
  1 cucumber, peeled, seeded,
    and diced
  1 pimiento half, chopped
  2 hard-cooked egg yolks

1 teaspoon Dijon mustard
½ cup mild olive oil, or ¼ cup
  olive oil and ¼ cup vegetable
  oil
¼ cup red wine vinegar
  Dash of Tabasco sauce
  Salt and pepper to taste
2 hard-cooked egg whites,
  chopped, for garnish

Boil potatoes in their skins in water to cover until just tender. Drain into colander; then, while still hot, hold under cold running water and slip off skin. Slice and place in a large bowl. Add green onion, celery, and beef. Toss lightly to mix. Add pickle, cucumber, and pimiento. Set aside at room temperature.

In a small bowl, mash the egg yolks with the mustard until smooth. Stir in the oil and vinegar. Add Tabasco, salt, and pepper. Beat with a fork until smooth. Pour over salad and toss to mix. Chop the egg whites and sprinkle over the salad as garnish.

Makes 6 servings.

GERMAN-STYLE HOT POTATO SALAD

This classic recipe has never lost its appeal.

2½–3 pounds medium potatoes	1 teaspoon salt
4 slices bacon	1 tablespoon sugar
¼ cup finely chopped onion	½ cup water
1 tablespoon flour	1 egg
1 teaspoon dry mustard	¼ cup vinegar

Scrub potatoes under cold running water, then drop them into a large pan of rapidly boiling water, enough to cover by about 2 inches. Cook at a brisk simmer until sufficiently tender to pierce with the point of a small knife. Drain into colander. Hold potatoes 1 at a time under running water and slip off skin. Slice immediately into ½-inch rounds, letting rounds fall into a large bowl. Set aside.

Cook bacon in a large, heavy skillet until crisp. Drain on paper toweling and chop into small pieces. Pour off all but 2 tablespoons of bacon fat from skillet and stir in onion. Cook until golden brown. Blend in flour, mustard, salt, and sugar. When smooth, stir in water and cook, stirring, 1–2 minutes.

Place egg in a bowl and beat until blended. Stir in about 2 tablespoons of hot mixture, then add remaining hot mixture. Blend in vinegar. Pour over still-hot potatoes. Sprinkle with chopped bacon.

If desired, serve with pumpernickel bread with whipped butter.

Makes 4 servings.

POTATO AND BELGIAN ENDIVE SALAD

Here is another version of French potato salad to add to your list of picnic fare.

2½–3 small new potatoes
  2 tablespoons olive oil
  2 tablespoons white wine vinegar, or to taste
  Salt to taste
  Freshly ground black pepper to taste
2–3 medium to large Belgian endives

¾ cup mayonnaise, preferably homemade (see page 181)
¼ cup minced parsley
¼ cup minced chives or green onion
Sliced hard-cooked eggs for garnish (optional)

Scrub potatoes under cold running water. Place in a large pan of lightly salted water, bring to a boil, and let boil until sufficiently cooked to pierce easily with a small, sharp knife. Hold potatoes 1 at a time under cold running water and slip off skin. Cut into thick slices or chunks, letting slices or chunks fall into a large bowl. Add oil and vinegar. Season to taste with salt and pepper. Set aside at room temperature, tossing occasionally or until almost all liquid has been absorbed.

Trim endives and, if necessary, remove and discard damaged outer leaves. Cut each across into ¼-inch-thick rounds and add them to the potatoes. Add mayonnaise, parsley, and chives. Use 2 forks to toss salad, being careful not to break up or mash the potatoes. Transfer to a serving bowl and, if you like, garnish with egg slices.

If desired, serve with Creole-Style Hot and Spicy Cheese Rounds (see page 170).
Makes 6 servings.

POTATO SALAD ALMONDINE

Crisp almond slivers and small red potatoes combine to give this old favorite fresh appeal.

Almondine Dressing (see
below)
2½-3 pounds small red potatoes
2 tablespoons Vinaigrette
Dressing (see page 174)
5-6 green onions, trimmed and
chopped
1 small green pepper, cut into
thin strips

½ cup minced parsley
2 stalks celery, trimmed and
thinly sliced
¼ cup chopped green olives
Salt and pepper to taste
Slivered almonds for garnish
(optional)

ALMONDINE DRESSING
Peanut or vegetable oil
½ cup slivered almonds
Salt

2 tablespoons lemon juice
½ cup mayonnaise

To prepare Almondine Dressing: Pour 2 tablespoons of oil into a small skillet over medium high heat. When hot, add almonds and cook, stirring, until crisp and light golden in color. Remove with slotted spoon and drain on paper toweling. Set aside. In a medium bowl, combine 1 teaspoon of salt, lemon juice, mayonnaise, and 1-2 teaspoons of oil. Beat until light and creamy. Fold in almonds. Taste and add additional salt, if desired. Set aside.

Fill a large pot with water and bring to a full boil over high heat. Add potatoes, lower heat, partially cover pot, and let simmer until tender but not falling apart. Drain into colander. Do not peel. Cut into chunks and transfer to a large bowl. Add Vinaigrette Dressing, green onions, pepper, parsley, celery, and olives. Add Almondine Dressing and toss to mix ingredients thoroughly. Add salt and pepper to taste. Spoon into a large salad bowl. Let stand at room temperature until ready to serve. Sprinkle with almonds, if desired.

Makes 4-6 servings.

POTATO AND MARINATED BEEF SALAD

You can use leftover roast beef for this salad. Since there is very seldom leftover roast beef at our house, however, we use rare roast beef from the "deli." It makes a hearty, flavorful, and special salad that is expensive but worth every bite.

Mayonnaise Vinaigrette
Dressing (see below)
1 *pound medium rare roast*
  beef
2 *tablespoons soy sauce*
2 *tablespoons red wine vine-*
  gar
2 *tablespoons peanut or vege-*
  table oil

2½–3 *pounds medium-size new*
  potatoes, all approximately
  the same size
1 *small green pepper, seeded*
  and chopped
1 *small purple onion, chopped*
½ *cup minced parsley*
  Crisp lettuce leaves

MAYONNAISE VINAIGRETTE DRESSING
1 *teaspoon coarse salt*
½ *teaspoon freshly ground*
  black pepper
2 *tablespoons wine vinegar*

6 *tablespoons mild olive oil or*
  vegetable oil
2 *tablespoons prepared*
  mayonnaise

To prepare Mayonnaise Vinaigrette Dressing: In a small bowl, combine salt, pepper, and vinegar. Add oil in a slow, steady stream, beating as added. Beat in mayonnaise. Correct seasoning with additional salt and pepper if desired. Set aside.

If buying the beef from a delicatessen, have it cut into thick slices. At home, cut slices into julienne strips. Place strips in a long, shallow, nonmetal baking dish and pour over them the soy sauce, vinegar, and oil. Toss lightly to mix. Set aside for about 1 hour, or cover and refrigerate for several hours, but bring to room temperature before using.

Cook potatoes in a large pot of boiling water until tender but not falling apart. Drain into colander, then, while still hot, hold potatoes 1 at a time under cold running water and slip off skin. Cut into bite-size chunks, letting chunks fall into a large bowl. Add green pepper, onion, and parsley. Pour on the Mayonnaise Vinaigrette Dressing and toss to mix thoroughly. Drain, add the beef, and toss again. Spoon salad onto lettuce-lined plates or into a large lettuce-lined bowl. Serve at room temperature.

Makes 4 servings.

POTATO SALAD WITH CUCUMBERS AND PIMIENTO

For this salad the potatoes and cucumber are marinated in a mild vinaigrette until they are seasoned all the way through. They are then combined with a flavorful sour cream mayonnaise and pimiento.

2½–3 pounds small new or red potatoes
3 tablespoons olive oil
1 tablespoon white wine vinegar
1 small cucumber, peeled,
 halved, seeded, and cut into
 narrow shapes
Salt to taste
½ cup mayonnaise, preferably
 homemade (see page 181)

½ cup sour cream or yogurt
1 tablespoon fresh lemon juice
½ small red onion, chopped
1 tablespoon chopped fresh
 basil leaves, or ½ teaspoon
 dried basil
Pepper to taste
½ pimiento, cut into narrow
 strips

Place potatoes in a large pan of boiling water and boil until tender but not falling apart. Transfer into colander and rinse quickly with warm water. Hold potatoes 1 at a time over a large bowl and cut into wedges or thick slices. Add olive oil, vinegar, cucumber, and salt. Cover and refrigerate several hours or overnight. Drain and transfer to a large bowl.

In a small bowl, combine mayonnaise and sour cream. Stir in lemon juice. Add onion and basil. Season with salt and pepper to taste. Spoon over potato-cucumber mixture. Add pimiento. Toss lightly with 2 forks to combine ingredients. Serve at room temperature.

Makes 4 servings.

POTATO SALAD CREOLE-STYLE

This is our adaptation of a recipe found in a small cookbook in New Orleans that was first published over 100 years ago.

Creole Dressing (see below)
2 tablespoons peanut or vegetable oil
1 tablespoon red wine vinegar
½ teaspoon salt
¼ teaspoon coarsely ground black pepper
2⅓–3 pounds very small new potatoes, all approximately the same size

1 small green pepper, trimmed, seeded, and chopped
1–2 small stalks celery, chopped
½ cup minced green onion
Hard-cooked egg wedges and chopped dill pickle for garnish (optional)

CREOLE DRESSING

1 egg
1 egg yolk
¾ cup peanut or vegetable oil
2 tablespoons red wine vinegar

1 teaspoon Creole-style mustard
2–3 dashes of Tabasco sauce
Salt and pepper to taste

To prepare Creole Dressing: Place egg and egg yolk in the bowl of a food processor or blender and process or blend until well mixed and frothy. With the machine on, slowly add the oil in a thin, steady stream. Add remaining ingredients and process or blend until mixed. If desired, cover and refrigerate until about 30 minutes before using. Set aside.

In a large bowl, combine the oil, vinegar, salt, and black pepper and whisk with a fork until well blended. In a large saucepan, cover potatoes with water and bring to a full boil. Lower heat slightly and let cook at a brisk simmer until tender. Drain. While still hot, hold potatoes 1 at a time over bowl with oil-vinegar mixture and cut each into 4 wedges, letting wedges fall into bowl. Toss lightly to mix and let stand about 15 minutes. Add green pepper, celery, and green onion. Mix in Creole Dressing. Transfer to a serving bowl and garnish, if desired, with egg wedges and dill pickle.

If desired, serve with Pickled Shrimp (see page 158).

Makes 6 servings.

POTATO SALAD WITH GREEN BEANS AND TURKEY

This is one of the best ways I know to make use of that leftover holiday bird.

2½–3 pounds small new potatoes, unpeeled and well scrubbed
½ cup Vinaigrette Dressing (see page 174)
1 pound green snap beans, trimmed
1 pound cooked turkey, both white and dark meat, diced

1 small can anchovy filets, drained
2 tablespoons chopped fresh basil leaves, or ½ teaspoon dried basil
Crisp lettuce leaves
Tomatoes, quartered or thinly sliced, for garnish

Boil potatoes in their skins in lightly salted water to cover until just tender. Drain into colander; while still hot, hold potatoes 1 at a time over a large bowl and cut into thick slices, letting slices fall into bowl. Add ¼ cup Vinaigrette Dressing and toss to mix. Set aside at room temperature.

Place green beans on steamer rack over simmering water, cover, and steam until crisp-tender. Drain and add to potatoes. Add remaining Vinaigrette Dressing and other ingredients and toss to mix. Transfer to a lettuce-lined bowl or salad plates. If desired, garnish with tomatoes. **Makes 4–6 servings.**

SCANDINAVIAN POTATO SALAD

No Scandinavian smorgasbord would be complete without at least one mixed potato and vegetable salad. This easy-to-prepare version can also be served as a light main-course luncheon dish.

Sour Cream Horseradish
 Dressing (see below)
2½–3 pounds boiling potatoes
 ¼ cup Vinaigrette Dressing (see
  page 174)
2–3 medium-size carrots,
  scraped, trimmed, and cut
  into ½-inch cubes
1 cup tiny frozen peas, thawed
1 large tart apple, cored and
  chopped
1 8-ounce can diced beets,
  drained
1 small Vidalia or other mild,
  sweet onion, chopped
 Salt to taste
 Coarsely ground black pepper to taste
 Marinated herring, well
  drained and cut into thin
  strips, for garnish (optional)

SOUR CREAM HORSERADISH DRESSING
 ½ cup mayonnaise, preferably
  homemade (see recipe 181)
 ½ cup sour cream

1–2 tablespoons prepared horse-
  radish
 Salt and pepper to taste
 Fresh lemon juice (optional)

To prepare Sour Cream Horseradish Dressing: In a medium bowl, combine mayonnaise, sour cream, and horseradish. Season with salt and pepper to taste. If desired, thin dressing with lemon juice. Cover and refrigerate until ready to use.

In a large pot, boil potatoes in water to cover until tender. Drain into colander, cool slightly, then peel and cut into small cubes. Place in a large bowl, add Vinaigrette Dressing, and toss lightly to mix. Set aside at room temperature.

Cook carrots in boiling water to cover until just tender, then drain. Add carrots and peas to potato mixture. If desired, mixture can be set aside at room temperature until ready to complete salad.

Just before serving, add apple, beets, and onion to potato mixture. Season with salt and pepper to taste. Add Sour Cream Horseradish Dressing and toss to mix. Transfer to a serving bowl and, if desired, top with strips of marinated herring.

Makes 6 servings.

RUSSIAN POTATO SALAD WITH PICKLED BEETS AND SOUR CREAM DRESSING

If you're fond of potato salads, I think you'll like this version with its surprise addition of pickled beets. It is elegant served on a platter lined with crisp lettuce and surrounded with garnishes.

¼ cup Vinaigrette Dressing (see page 174)
  Sour Cream Mayonnaise Dressing (see below)
2½–3 pounds boiling potatoes
  ¼ cup minced chives
  1 medium-size cucumber
  1 small dill pickle, chopped

1 8-ounce can pickled beets, drained
  Crisp lettuce leaves
  Chopped smoked salmon (optional), chopped hard-cooked eggs, chopped onion, and capers for garnish

SOUR CREAM MAYONNAISE DRESSING
  1 tablespoon peanut or vegetable oil
  1 tablespoon white wine vinegar
  1 tablespoon Dijon mustard

¼ cup mayonnaise, preferably homemade (see page 181)
½ cup sour cream
  Salt and pepper to taste

Prepare Vinaigrette Dressing and set aside. To prepare Sour Cream Mayonnaise Dressing: In a medium bowl, combine oil, vinegar, and mustard. Beat with a fork until well mixed. Add mayonnaise and sour cream and beat until mixture is smooth. Season with salt and pepper to taste. Set aside.

Place potatoes in a large pot of boiling water; lower heat slightly and let simmer until tender. Drain into colander. Hold hot potatoes 1 at a time under cold running water and slip off skin; cut into thick slices and place in a large bowl. Add Vinaigrette Dressing and chives. Toss lightly to mix and set aside at room temperature. If desired, potatoes may be prepared ahead to this point. Cover lightly and let stand at room temperature until ready to use.

Peel cucumber, cut lengthwise in half, and scoop out seeds. Cut halves into thin slices and add to potato mixture. Add chopped pickles and beets. Add Sour Cream Mayonnaise Dressing and toss lightly to mix ingredients.

Spoon salad onto a lettuce-lined platter. Sprinkle with chopped smoked salmon, if desired, and surround with remaining garnishes.
Makes 6 servings.

Salade Niçoise

In restaurants up and down the Mediterranean coast we found many different versions of this famous salad. Each, we were told, was the original and, of course, the best. Here are 2 versions, a classic and an American adaptation. We think you'll like them both.

CLASSIC SALADE NIÇOISE

1 pound tender young green beans
½ cup Vinaigrette Dressing (see page 174)
2½–3 pounds very small new potatoes, all approximately the same size
Crisp lettuce leaves
2 7-ounce cans imported solid-pack tuna in olive oil, drained and flaked

2 large ripe tomatoes, cut into wedges
2 hard-cooked eggs, cut into wedges
1 2-ounce can caper-stuffed anchovy filets, drained
2 tablespoons chopped green onions
½ cup Niçoise olives for garnish

Cook beans in a large pot of rapidly boiling water until crisp-tender. Drain and transfer to a large storage bowl; add ¼ cup of Vinaigrette Dressing, cover, and refrigerate until ready to use. Drain just before using.

In a second pot, cook potatoes in boiling water until tender but not falling apart. Drain and cut into wedges while still hot, dropping wedges into a bowl. Toss with remaining Vinaigrette Dressing.

Arrange lettuce on 4–6 large salad plates. Place a mound of tuna in the center of each, dividing evenly. Arrange beans and then potatoes around each mound of tuna. Surround potatoes with tomato and egg wedges. Top each mound of tuna with anchovy filets. Sprinkle with green onions and garnish with olives.

If desired, serve with Brushette.

Makes 4–6 servings.

SALADE NIÇOISE AMERICAN-STYLE

This one is quick, easy, elegant and, of course, delicious.

3–4 pounds very small new potatoes, all approximately the
  same size
⅓ cup mild olive oil
1 tablespoon red wine vinegar
½ teaspoon salt
  Sprinkling of coarsely ground
  black pepper
1 1-pound can 3-bean salad,
  drained

2 7-ounce cans solid-pack white
  tuna, drained and separated
  into chunks
½ cup coarsely chopped pitted
  Niçoise olives
  Crisp lettuce leaves
1–2 tablespoons mayonnaise (optional)

In a large pot, boil potatoes in water to cover until tender but not falling apart. Drain, cut into thick slices or chunks while still warm, and
place in a large bowl. Add oil, vinegar, salt, and pepper. Toss to mix.
Add bean salad, tuna, and olives. Toss lightly. Spoon into lettuce-lined
bowl. If desired, top with a bit of mayonnaise.
Makes 4–6 servings.

Shoestring potato and carrot salad

Here is a very different potato salad with a crunchy texture.

1 cup shredded carrots
¼ cup sliced scallions
½ cup mayonnaise, homemade
  (see page 181) or store-bought
1 cup diced celery
8 ounces chicken, cooked,
  skinned, boned, and diced, or 1
  7½-ounce can tuna, drained and
  flaked

1 can shoestring potatoes
  Freshly ground black pepper to
  taste

In a medium bowl, mix together carrots, scallions, mayonnaise, celery,
and chicken. Cover and refrigerate until ready to use (at least 2 hours
or overnight).
  Just before serving add shoestring potatoes and place in a serving
bowl. Sprinkle with pepper.
Makes 4–6 servings.

Salade brimont

This adaptation from the *Larousse Gastronomique* is even better than the original. It's very French but very easy to prepare.

3–4 *pounds small new potatoes, each about 3 inches in diameter*
2 *tablespoons olive oil*
2 *teaspoons sherry wine vinegar*
1 *teaspoon salt*
   Coarsely ground black pepper to taste
1 *pound canned artichoke hearts, drained and sliced*

1 *cup Curried Mayonnaise Dressing (see page 32)*
1 *6–8-ounce package frozen cooked "popcorn" shrimp, thawed*
6–8 *Niçoise olives*
  ¼ *cup chopped parsley*
   Hard-cooked egg wedges

Cook potatoes in water to cover until tender. Drain into colander, then cut into wedges while still hot, letting wedges fall into a large bowl. Add oil, vinegar, salt, pepper, and artichoke hearts. Toss lightly to mix.

Transfer salad to an attractive serving bowl. Use a spatula or the back of a spoon to cover completely with a thin layer of Curried Mayonnaise Dressing. Top with shrimp, olives, and parsley. Arrange egg wedges around edge of bowl.

Makes 6–8 servings.

SWEET POTATO SALAD WITH AIOLI DRESSING

Sound mundane? Don't you believe it. This is positively the most elegant and flavorful salad you could possibly prepare.

Aioli Dressing (see below)
2 medium to large round or oblong sweet potatoes
1 tablespoon peanut or vegetable oil
2 medium carrots, scraped and cut at a 45-degree angle into thin, oval slices
8 ounces tender young snap green beans, trimmed

3–4 stalks broccoli, cut into flowerets
1 teaspoon salt
1 pound filet of cod
1–2 ounces anchovy filets, drained and chopped
½ cup coarsely chopped pitted Niçoise olives
2 hard-cooked eggs, quartered, for garnish (optional)

AIOLI DRESSING

1 egg yolk
4 cloves garlic, peeled and coarsely chopped
1 tablespoon Dijon mustard

½ teaspoon salt
¾ cup olive oil
½ cup fresh lemon juice
Salt to taste

Preheat oven to 400 degrees Fahrenheit.

To prepare Aioli Dressing: Place egg yolk, garlic, mustard, and salt in the bowl of a food processor or blender and process until blended. With the motor running, add half of the olive oil in a thin steady stream. When the mixture is smooth add half of the lemon juice and process or blend until mixed. Add the remaining oil and lemon juice and season with salt. Process or blend to a smooth, thin mayonnaise-like mixture. Transfer to a medium serving bowl. Refrigerate until ready to serve.

Bake sweet potatoes until soft, around 30–45 minutes. Let cool slightly, then peel and cut into thick slices. Set aside.

Pour oil into a large, heavy skillet or wok over high heat. When oil is hot add carrots and stir-fry about 1 minute. Add green beans and stir-fry until crisp-tender. Stir in broccoli flowerets and stir-fry 30 seconds more. Transfer all the vegetables to a large bowl and set aside.

Place about ½ cup of water in a large skillet; add salt and bring to a boil. Add fish filets in a single layer. Lower heat so water simmers and cook until fish filets are opaque through center. Use a spatula to transfer filets to paper toweling. Drain slightly, then break up into large chunks.

Arrange vegetables on a large round or oval platter. Sprinkle evenly with about 2 tablespoons of Aioli Dressing. Arrange cod in the center of the platter. Scatter with anchovies and olives. Garnish, if desired, with the hard-cooked eggs. Serve remaining Aioli Dressing separately to spoon over each serving.

Makes 4–6 servings.

ALEXANDRE DUMAS POTATO SALADE FRANÇAISE

A French classic updated.

3 pounds small new potatoes, all
   approximately the same size
¼ cup dry white wine
½ cup fruity olive oil
2 tablespoons white wine vinegar
1 teaspoon dry mustard

1 teaspoon salt
   Freshly ground black pepper to
   taste
¼ cup finely chopped scallions
¼ cup finely minced parsley

Scrub potatoes under cold running water, then drop into a large pan of rapidly boiling water, enough to cover by about 2 inches. Let cook at a brisk simmer until sufficiently tender to pierce with the point of a small knife. Drain into colander. Let cool slightly, then hold potatoes 1 at a time over a large bowl and cut into small chunks, letting chunks fall into bowl. Pour in wine and stir the cubes very gently with a rubber spatula until thoroughly moistened. Let stand for 15–20 minutes.

In a small bowl, combine oil, vinegar, dry mustard, and salt. Beat with a fork until blended and smooth. Add pepper. Pour over potatoes. Add remaining ingredients and toss lightly again to combine. Serve at room temperature.

Makes 4–6 servings.

GLORIOUS BEAN SALADS

5.

But beans are fattening, aren't they? The answer is yes and no. Though old-fashioned baked beans made with salt pork and brown sugar or molasses are certainly off limits when you're watching your weight, a great-tasting main-course bean salad with vegetables is so wonderfully satisfying, so filled with good nutrition, it can actually help you lose those unwanted pounds.

With the exception of a green bean salad—which to my way of thinking is worth making only with crisp, freshly cooked beans—you can use either canned or cooked dried beans.

To Prepare Canned Beans for Salads

Place ½–1 pound beans into colander and rinse with very hot water until water runs clear. Blot beans dry and transfer to a large bowl. Add 1 tablespoon of top-quality extra-virgin olive oil and 2 teaspoons of vinegar—the same vinegar you're going to use in your salad. Toss to mix and let stand at room temperature for about 30 minutes. Prepare salad as directed in recipe.

To Cook Dried Beans for Salads

Soak beans in water to cover for 12–16 hours or place in a saucepan and cover by about 2 inches with water. Bring to a full boil and boil about 2 minutes, then remove pan from heat and let beans stand in water for 1 hour—no longer. Drain before cooking. Place ½–1 pound prepared beans in a large saucepan and cover by about 2 inches with fresh water. Add 1 small peeled and quartered onion, 1 bay leaf and, if desired, 1–2 cloves of crushed garlic. Bring to a boil, then lower heat and let simmer until just tender but not mushy. (Cooking time depends on age and type of bean.) Stir in about 1 teaspoon of salt and continue to simmer for about 1 minute. Drain beans into colander, let cool slightly, then remove and discard onion, bay leaf, and garlic, if used. If desired, transfer beans to a storage bowl, cover, and refrigerate until ready to prepare salad. Remove from refrigerator about 30 minutes before using.

BEAN SALAD PENNSYLVANIA DUTCH-STYLE

This salad is even better when prepared ahead.

1 8-ounce carton sour cream
2 tablespoons apple cider vinegar
1 tablespoon brown sugar
2 teaspoons horseradish
  Salt and pepper to taste
1 15–16-ounce can lima beans, rinsed and drained
1 15–16-ounce can red kidney beans, rinsed and drained

1 15–16-ounce can cannellini beans, rinsed and drained
1 small Italian (purple) onion, chopped
½ cup chopped sweet mixed pickles
¼ cup minced parsley
2 cups shredded Chinese cabbage or iceberg lettuce

Place sour cream, vinegar, sugar, horseradish, salt, and pepper in a large bowl. Whisk until sugar and salt have dissolved. Add beans, onion, pickles, and parsley. Lift and toss salad to mix thoroughly. Cover and refrigerate (4–24 hours) until about 30 minutes before serving. When ready to serve, add lettuce, toss to mix, then transfer to a large serving bowl.

Makes 6–8 servings.

BEAN SALAD WITH TUNA AND CAVIAR

This salad is not only elegant it's positively aristocratic!

⅓ cup top-quality extra-virgin
olive oil
1 tablespoon white wine or tarragon vinegar
½ teaspoon salt
Freshly ground black pepper to
taste
¼ cup finely chopped scallions or
green onions
1 15–16-ounce can cannellini
beans

½ cup finely chopped celery
1 7-ounce can imported Italian
tuna in olive oil, drained
¼ cup finely minced parsley
2 tablespoons or 1 2-ounce jar red
salmon caviar
Crisp lettuce leaves
Lemon wedges for garnish

In a large bowl, combine oil, vinegar, salt, and pepper. Beat with a fork until blended. Stir in scallions.

Rinse beans in colander with hot water until water runs clear. Blot dry and add to oil-vinegar mixture. Toss lightly with fork. Set aside for about 30 minutes, tossing beans occasionally so that they absorb some of the oil-vinegar mixture. Add celery.

Break tuna into small chunks and add to bean mixture. Add parsley and caviar. Toss to mix.

To serve, spoon salad onto lettuce-lined plates and garnish with lemon wedges.

Makes 4–6 servings.

Bean Salad with Smoked Fish

Here is a hearty and satisfying salad to serve with rye bread and butter sandwiches. Cold beer is a perfect accompaniment.

Horseradish Mayonnaise Dressing (see below)
8 ounces green snap beans
1 15–16-ounce can red kidney beans

½ small red onion, chopped
8 ounces smoked mackerel or other smoked fish, skinned and boned
2 hard-cooked eggs, chopped

HORSERADISH MAYONNAISE DRESSING
½ cup sour cream
½ cup mayonnaise, preferably homemade (see page 181)
2 tablespoons horseradish
¼ cup chopped radishes
Dash of Tabasco sauce
Salt to taste
Coarsely ground black pepper to taste

To prepare Horseradish Mayonnaise Dressing: Combine all ingredients and mix well. Set aside.

Trim and wash green beans. Place on rack in steamer pot over simmering water; cover and steam until crisp-tender, 8–10 minutes (or cook beans in a pot of rapidly boiling water until crisp-tender). Drain into colander, then immediately rinse under cold water to stop cooking process. Blot dry and place in a large bowl. Add red beans and chopped onions. Stir in Horseradish Mayonnaise Dressing. Carefully fold in fish and hard-cooked eggs. If desired, cover and refrigerate until about 30 minutes before serving.

Makes 4–6 servings.

Bean salad with tuna

This is an easy recipe. With ingredients on hand this salad can be put together in a matter of minutes. It's a great way to extend your menu for unexpected guests.

1 7½-ounce can tuna packed in oil
1 15–16-ounce can cannellini beans
1 1-pound can green bean salad, drained
2–3 stalks celery, cut across at a 45-degree angle into thin slices
½ cup minced parsley
2 tablespoons chopped fresh basil leaves, or 1 teaspoon dried basil

1 tablespoon red wine vinegar
½ cup mayonnaise, preferably homemade (see page 181)
Salt and pepper to taste
Crisp lettuce leaves
Niçoise olives, sliced or coarsely chopped, and parsley sprigs for garnish (optional)

Place undrained tuna in a large bowl and break up with a fork. Add cannellini beans and bean salad mixture. Toss lightly. Add celery, parsley, and basil.

In a small bowl, combine vinegar and mayonnaise. Add to salad and toss to mix thoroughly. Season to taste with salt and pepper. If desired, refrigerate until about 30 minutes before serving. Transfer to a lettuce-lined bowl and, if you wish, sprinkle surface of salad with olives and surround bowl with parsley sprigs. If desired, serve with Marinated Cucumbers (see page 158).

Makes 6 servings.

BRAZILIAN BLACK BEAN SALAD

If a salad could be called seductive, this Brazilian classic is the one.

1 8-ounce package dried black
  beans
Salt
2 tablespoons corn, peanut, or
  vegetable oil
3 cloves garlic
1 large carrot, scraped and
  chopped
1 large purple onion, chopped
2 stalks celery, chopped
1 small green pepper, chopped
1 teaspoon ground coriander

½ teaspoon ground cumin
1 large navel orange, peeled and
  sectioned
1 tablespoon sherry wine vinegar
1 teaspoon fresh lemon juice
  Coarsely ground black pepper
  to taste
1 small head Boston or Bibb lettuce, torn into bite-size chunks
1 8-ounce carton sour cream or
  yogurt

Rinse beans under cold running water, then place in a large bowl.
Cover with water and let stand for several hours or overnight. Drain
into colander and place in a large pan. Cover by about 2 inches of
water and bring to a full boil. Lower heat, partially cover pot, and let
beans simmer for about 1 hour. Add 2 teaspoons of salt and continue
to simmer until beans are tender. Drain and place in a large bowl.

Pour oil into a large skillet over low heat. Add garlic and cook, stirring occasionally, until very tender. Remove and discard garlic, add
carrot, and stir for 1 minute. Add onion, celery, and green pepper. Stir
in coriander and cumin. Scrape mixture over beans in bowl.

Holding each orange section over a medium bowl, cut in half, letting
pieces and juice fall into bowl. Add vinegar, lemon juice, pepper and, if
desired, a small amount of salt. Add to bean-vegetable mixture. Toss to
mix. Refrigerate, if desired, until about 30 minutes before serving. Stir
in lettuce chunks, then transfer to a serving bowl. Serve chilled sour
cream or yogurt separately.

Makes 6–8 servings.

Bulgur salad

The crunchy texture and nutlike flavor of bulgur mixed with crisp vegetables and accented by lemony dressing make this salad irresistibly good.

1 small lemon
2 tablespoons sugar
1 cup bulgur wheat
1 teaspoon salt
2 cups boiling water
1 15–16-ounce can red kidney
  beans

1 small red onion, chopped
2 small zucchini, trimmed and
  chopped
¼ cup minced parsley
½ cup raisins
  Lemony Vinaigrette Dressing
  (see below)

LEMONY VINAIGRETTE DRESSING
  Juice of 1 small lemon (about 4
  tablespoons)
2 tablespoons red wine vinegar
1 teaspoon sugar
¼ teaspoon dried oregano, or 1 tablespoon chopped fresh oregano
  leaves

½ teaspoon dried basil
½ cup peanut or vegetable oil
  Salt and pepper to taste

Cut zest (yellow part of rind) from lemon and cut into julienne strips. Place in a small saucepan and cover with about 2 inches of water. Bring to a boil and stir in sugar. Lower heat and let simmer for about 10 minutes. Drain and blot strips thoroughly dry with paper toweling. Set aside.

Place bulgur in a large heat-proof bowl. Add salt and boiling water. Let stand at room temperature until all liquid is absorbed, about 30 minutes. Blot dry with paper toweling. Transfer to a serving bowl.

Drain beans into colander, then rinse under cold running water until water runs clear. Blot dry and add to bulgur wheat. Add onion, zucchini, parsley, and raisins. Drain and add lemon zest.

To prepare Lemony Vinaigrette Dressing: In a small bowl, combine lemon juice, vinegar, sugar, oregano, and basil. Stir to mix, then slowly add oil, beating as added. Season to taste with salt and pepper.

Stir in Lemony Vinaigrette Dressing and toss salad to mix thoroughly. Cover and refrigerate until chilled or ready to serve.

If desired, serve with Syrian-style bread rounds.

Makes 6–8 generous servings.

BULGUR SALAD WITH FRUITED RAITA

Raita is a combination of yogurt and vegetables or fruits, raw or cooked, plus fragrant and delicate seasonings. Combined with bulgur it makes a perfect salad for a Near Eastern-style meal.

1½ cups bulgur wheat
1 teaspoon salt
½ cup frozen peas, thawed and drained
1 small cucumber, seeded and chopped

¼ cup minced green onion
¼ cup minced parsley
1 small hot red pepper, seeded and minced
Fruited Raita (see below)
Salt and pepper to taste

FRUITED RAITA
1 tablespoon peanut or vegetable oil
1 teaspoon mustard seeds
¼ teaspoon cayenne pepper
2 medium-size tart, crisp apples, peeled, seeded, and coarsely grated

½ teaspoon salt
1 teaspoon sugar
1 8-ounce carton plain lowfat yogurt

To prepare Fruited Raita: In a small, heavy skillet over medium heat, pour oil, then add mustard seeds, stirring until they turn a light golden nut brown, 1–2 minutes. Stir in the cayenne. Remove from heat and add apples. Add salt, sugar, and yogurt. Beat with a fork to mix. Pour into a small bowl and refrigerate for several hours or until chilled.

In a large heat-proof bowl, combine bulgur and salt. Add sufficient boiling water to cover by about 2 inches. Let stand 25–30 minutes or until all water has been absorbed. Blot dry with paper towels. Transfer to a serving bowl. Add peas, cucumber, onion, parsley, and hot red pepper. Stir in Fruited Raita. Season to taste with salt and pepper. Cover and chill until ready to serve.

Makes 6–8 servings.

ITALIAN GREEN BEAN SALAD

It's impossible to give exact proportions per person for this salad; it's so good that most people eat more than expected.

3 pounds crisp fresh snap green
    beans, trimmed
1 small purple onion, chopped
    Italian Vinaigrette Dressing (see
    below)

1 large tomato
¼ cup grated Parmesan cheese
    Pitted Niçoise olives for garnish
    (optional)

ITALIAN VINAIGRETTE DRESSING
⅓ cup olive or vegetable oil (or
    half olive oil, half vegetable oil)
1 clove garlic, crushed
2 tablespoons chopped fresh basil
    leaves, or 1 teaspoon dried basil

1 teaspoon sugar
2 tablespoons red wine vinegar
    Salt to taste
    Coarsely ground black pepper
    to taste

In a large, heavy skillet, place beans and add water to cover by about ½ inch. Bring to a full boil, then lower heat and let simmer until crisp-tender. Drain into colander and blot dry. (If you wish, you can steam the beans instead.) Transfer to a large bowl and stir in onions.

To prepare Italian Vinaigrette Dressing: Pour oil into a large, heavy skillet over low heat. Add garlic and cook, stirring, until limp but not browned. Remove and discard garlic. Stir in basil and sugar. Stir until sugar has dissolved. Remove skillet from heat and stir in vinegar. Season with salt and pepper to taste. Pour over salad while still warm and toss to mix. Cover and refrigerate for 2–3 hours, or until 30 minutes before using.

Cut tomato in half and gently squeeze out all seeds and juice. Cut halves into narrow strips and blot dry. Transfer bean-onion mixture with slotted spoon onto individual lettuce-lined salad plates or a large bowl. Top with tomato strips and sprinkle with cheese. If desired, garnish with olives.

Makes 4–6 servings.

Hummus with Crudités

You can simplify a seated dinner party menu by serving this Near Eastern-style specialty as an appetizer along with pre-dinner drinks instead of serving a salad along with the meal.

HUMMUS

1 15–16-ounce can chick-peas
½ cup plain yogurt
3 tablespoons tahini (sesame seed paste)
3 tablespoons lemon juice

1 clove garlic, crushed
Salt
Coarsely ground black pepper to taste
Paprika for garnish (optional)

CRUDITÉS

1 cup broccoli flowerets
1 cup cauliflowerets
2 large carrots, trimmed and cut across at a 45-degree angle into thin oval shapes

1 small red bell pepper, seeded and cut into narrow strips
1 green bell pepper, seeded and cut into narrow strips
12 large mushrooms

To prepare Hummus: Place chick-peas into colander and rinse under cold water until water runs clear. Place in the bowl of a food processor and add approximately 2 tablespoons water, yogurt, tahini, and lemon juice. Process until smooth; add a little more water, if necessary, to make a thick, smooth mixture. Transfer to a medium bowl. Add garlic and season with salt and pepper. Cover bowl and refrigerate for several hours to allow flavors to mellow. Remove and discard garlic and, if desired, garnish with paprika.

To prepare Crudités: Place broccoli flowerets, cauliflowerets, carrot rounds, and bell peppers on a steamer rack over simmering water in a pot. Cover and let steam about 2 minutes. Transfer vegetables into colander and rinse briefly under cold running water to stop cooking process. Trim mushrooms and wipe clean with damp paper toweling.

To serve, transfer Hummus to medium serving bowl. Place bowl on a large round platter and surround with vegetables or spoon Hummus into 6 small bowls. Place each on a salad plate and circle with vegetables.

Makes 6 servings.

LATE-SUMMER BEAN SALAD WITH FRESH VEGETABLES

An inspired way to make use of the last cucumbers and zucchini from your garden.

1-2 medium to large cucumbers
(about 1 pound total weight)
1-2 medium to large zucchini
(about 1 pound total weight)
About 2 teaspoons salt
¼ cup white wine vinegar
1-2 medium to large ripe tomatoes
(about 1½ pounds total
weight)

1 small red onion, chopped
1 15–16-ounce can red kidney
beans, drained
⅓ cup Vinaigrette Dressing (see
page 174)
2 tablespoons chopped fresh
mint leaves
¼ cup minced parsley

Peel cucumbers, cut lengthwise in half, and scrape out seeds. Cut halves across into thin crescent shapes. Trim and dice zucchini into ¼–½-inch pieces. Place vegetables in a large bowl and sprinkle with about 2 teaspoons of salt. Add vinegar and toss to mix. Let stand at room temperature for about 30 minutes, then drain thoroughly.

Cut tomatoes in half and gently squeeze out all seeds and juice. Cut halves into narrow strips and blot thoroughly dry. Add to zucchini-cucumber mixture. Add onion and beans. Toss with Vinaigrette Dressing. Spoon into salad bowl and top with mint and parsley.

If desired, serve with Parsley Butter Fingers (see page 165).

Makes 4-6 servings.

LENTIL SALAD WITH CUCUMBER YOGURT DRESSING

This refreshing salad is a combination of garlic-flavored lentils, crisp, crunchy sun chokes, and a tangy cucumber yogurt dressing.

8 ounces sun chokes (Jerusalem
   artichokes)
2 cups dried lentils
3 cloves garlic, crushed
1 bay leaf
1 teaspoon salt
4 cups water
   Cucumber Yogurt Dressing (see
   below)

1 large tomato, seeded and
   chopped
¼ cup chopped green onion
¼ cup minced parsley
¼ cup chopped Sicilian-style green
   olives stuffed with peppers

CUCUMBER YOGURT DRESSING
1 small peeled cucumber
1 8-ounce carton plain yogurt or
   sour cream
2 teaspoons white wine vinegar
   or lemon juice

1 teaspoon sugar
   Salt
   Coarsely ground black pepper

To prepare Cucumber Yogurt Dressing: Coarsely grate cucumber over a small bowl. Stir in remaining ingredients. Set aside until ready to use or prepare ahead and refrigerate until about 30 minutes before using.

Wash sun chokes under cold running water, using hands to rub away any dirt. Trim off any soft or pink parts. Cut into small chunks. Place in a small bowl of cold water until ready to use.

In a large saucepan, combine lentils, garlic, bay leaf, salt, and water. Bring to a boil. Lower heat and let simmer for about 25 minutes. Add sun chokes. Continue to simmer for about 5 minutes or until lentils are tender. Drain into colander. Discard garlic and bay leaf. Pour lentil mixture into a large bowl. Stir in Cucumber Yogurt Dressing. Set aside until cool. Add remaining ingredients and toss to mix.

Makes 4–6 servings.

LENTIL SALAD WITH SOUR CREAM DRESSING

The earthy flavor of lentils combined with rich Sour Cream Dressing makes a splendid addition to a hearty buffet supper.

2 cups dried lentils
1 small white onion stuck with
  2 cloves
1 bay leaf
2 teaspoons salt
4-6 stalks celery, trimmed and cut
  across into thin crescent
  shapes

1 medium Vidalia onion, peeled
  and chopped
1 small green pepper, seeded
  and chopped
1 cup Sour Cream Dressing (see
  below)
  Minced parsley for garnish
  (optional)

SOUR CREAM DRESSING

1 cup sour cream
1 tablespoon white wine vinegar
1 teaspoon sugar

1 teaspoon Dijon or similar
  mustard
  Salt and pepper to taste

Place lentils in a large pot and cover with water by about 2 inches. Add white onion and bay leaf. Place over medium heat and let simmer about 20 minutes. Stir in salt. Continue to simmer until lentils are tender, about 15 minutes. Drain into colander. Remove and discard bay leaf and onion. Transfer to a large bowl. Stir in celery, Vidalia onion, and green pepper. Cool to room temperature.

To prepare Sour Cream Dressing: In a small bowl, combine sour cream, vinegar, sugar, and mustard. Beat until smooth. Add salt and pepper to taste.

Stir Sour Cream Dressing into lentils. If desired, sprinkle with minced parsley.

Makes 6-8 servings.

LENTIL SALAD WITH VINAIGRETTE AND CHOPPED WALNUTS

This make-ahead salad is great picnic fare.

Walnut Vinaigrette (see below)
2 cups dried lentils
1 clove garlic, crushed
½ small lemon, halved
1 small hot red chili pepper, trimmed, seeded, cut lengthwise, and halves cut into small slivers

½ teaspoon salt
½ cup minced scallions or green onions
1 cup coarsely chopped walnuts
Minced scallions or parsley for garnish (optional)

WALNUT VINAIGRETTE DRESSING
2 tablespoons white wine vinegar
½ cup walnut oil
1 clove garlic, peeled and coarsely chopped

Salt to taste
Coarsely ground black pepper to taste

To make Walnut Vinaigrette Dressing: Combine ingredients and blend well. Season to taste with salt and pepper. Set aside.

Place lentils in a large pot and cover with water by about 2 inches. Add garlic, lemon, and hot pepper. Bring to a boil over medium heat. Lower to a simmer, partly cover pot, and let cook for 20 minutes. Stir in salt and continue to cook until tender but still firm. Drain into colander, then transfer to a large bowl. Remove and discard lemon, garlic, and hot pepper. Gently stir Walnut Vinaigrette Dressing into lentils. Add scallions and chopped walnuts. Toss gently to mix. Cover bowl and refrigerate for several hours or overnight. Transfer to a serving bowl and sprinkle generously with minced scallions or parsley, if desired.

Makes 6–8 servings.

RED BEAN SALAD WITH MUSHROOMS

This salad is even better if made ahead. Just "hold" the mushrooms and lettuce, then add them right before serving.

Vinaigrette Dressing with Pickles (see below)
1 *15–16-ounce can red kidney beans, drained, rinsed, and blotted dry, or 2 cups home-cooked red kidney beans (see page 126)*
1 *small Vidalia onion, chopped*

¼ *cup minced parsley*
¼ *cup minced fresh basil leaves, or 3 tablespoons dried basil*
8 *ounces large mushrooms, trimmed and cut in T-shape slices*
2 *cups shredded romaine lettuce*

VINAIGRETTE DRESSING WITH PICKLES
3 *tablespoons white wine vinegar*
½ *cup fruity olive oil*
1 *tablespoon finely minced chives*
2 *teaspoons finely chopped cornichons or sour pickles*

Salt to taste
Coarsely ground black pepper to taste

To prepare Vinaigrette Dressing with Pickles: In medium bowl, combine all ingredients and beat with a fork until blended. Set aside.

In a large bowl, combine beans, onion, parsley, and basil. Add the Vinaigrette Dressing with Pickles and toss to mix. If desired, cover and refrigerate for several hours or overnight. Remove from refrigerator about 30 minutes before using. Add mushrooms and lettuce. Toss to mix.

Makes 4–6 servings.

BEAN AND ROTELLE SALAD

This hearty main-course salad looks as great as it tastes.

8 ounces rotelle
1 15–16-ounce can cannellini
   beans (white kidney beans)
¼ cup Vinaigrette Dressing
   (see page 174)
1 small green pepper
1 large ripe tomato
12–14 large romaine lettuce leaves

4 heaping tablespoons
   mayonnaise, preferably
   homemade (see page 181)
1 tablespoon fresh lemon
   juice (optional)
½ teaspoon salt or to taste
Black pepper to taste

Cook rotelle following directions on page 26. Drain and place in a large bowl. Drain beans into colander and hold under cold running water until water runs clear. Blot dry and add to pasta. Pour in Vinaigrette Dressing and toss lightly to mix. Set aside at room temperature for about 30 minutes.

Cut pepper into julienne strips. Cut tomato in half and squeeze halves to remove all seeds and juice. Cut into narrow strips and blot thoroughly dry. Cut lettuce across into thin strips and cut strips into 1-inch lengths. Add green pepper, tomato, and lettuce to pasta-bean mixture. Toss lightly to mix.

In a small bowl, combine mayonnaise, lemon juice (if desired), salt, and pepper. Pour over salad mixture. Toss to combine ingredients thoroughly. If desired, refrigerate salad until about 30 minutes before serving. Spoon into serving bowl or onto 6 salad plates.

If desired, serve with assorted finger sandwiches.

Makes 6 servings.

TACO SALAD HOME-STYLE

Would a girl from Texas write a book on salads without this recipe? Of course not. But is it gourmet? It is if you're from the Lone Star State.

2 cups shredded iceberg lettuce
½ cup chopped radishes
1 small green pepper, chopped
1 15–16-ounce can red kidney beans
1 tablespoon red wine vinegar
2–3 dashes of Tabasco sauce
1 tablespoon spicy hot catsup
Salt and pepper to taste

¼ cup peanut or vegetable oil
1 clove garlic, split
8 ounces lean ground beef
8 ounces Monterey Jack cheese, cubed
1 small Vidalia or other mild onion, chopped
1 small package taco chips

In a large bowl, combine lettuce, radishes, and green pepper. Cover and refrigerate until chilled or until ready to use.

Drain beans into colander, then rinse under cold water until water runs clear. Transfer about ¼ cup of beans to a medium bowl and mash until smooth. Stir in vinegar, Tabasco sauce, and catsup. Add salt and pepper to taste. Set the mashed and whole beans aside.

Pour oil into a large, heavy skillet over low heat. Add garlic and cook, stirring occasionally, until light golden in color. Remove and discard garlic. Raise heat to high. Add meat and cook, chopping with the tip of a spatula, until no longer pink. Stir in mashed bean mixture and add whole beans. Cook, stirring, until hot.

Spoon chilled lettuce mixture onto 4 salad plates. Top each with bean mixture and then cheese and onion, dividing evenly. Surround each salad with taco chips. Serve at once.

Makes 4 servings.

TEX-MEX SALAD

Here is another hearty salad for those who have a palate for something slightly "south of the border."

French Dressing (see below)
1 tablespoon oil
1 pound lean round steak, cut across into narrow strips
1 medium-size yellow onion, chopped
1 15-16-ounce can Mexican chili beans or red kidney beans
1 large tomato, seeded and chopped
½ cup chopped celery (optional)

½ cup chopped green pepper (optional)
1 head crisp iceberg lettuce, shredded or torn
8 ounces cheddar cheese, medium sharp to sharp, grated
1 avocado, peeled and cut into bite-size pieces
6–7-ounce package Mexican-flavored corn chips

FRENCH DRESSING
¼ cup sugar
¾ teaspoon dry mustard
½ teaspoon salt
½ teaspoon paprika
1 small yellow onion, grated
1 tablespoon lemon juice

½ cup catsup
¾ teaspoon Worcestershire sauce
2 tablespoons vinegar
2 tablespoons water
Dash of Tabasco
1 cup peanut or vegetable oil

To prepare French Dressing: Place all ingredients except oil in the bowl of a food processor or blender. Blend at low speed. With motor running, add oil in a slow, steady stream. Continue to blend until smooth. If desired, refrigerate until ready to use.

Pour oil into a large skillet over medium heat; when hot add meat and cook, stirring, until lightly browned. Stir in onion and cook until softened. Drain mixture into colander and blot with paper toweling. Set aside.

Put beans into colander and rinse until water runs clear. Prepare tomato, celery, and green pepper as directed. Set each aside in small separate bowls.

Place lettuce in a large salad bowl. Top with beans, tomato, celery, green pepper, and meat-onion mixture. Sprinkle with cheese. If desired, cover bowl and refrigerate until ready to complete salad. When

ready to serve top with avocado chunks and corn chips. Pour about half of dressing over top. Toss salad at the table just before serving. Serve remaining dressing separately.
Makes 6 servings.

THREE-BEAN SALAD WITH FILBERTS AND CREAMY VINAIGRETTE DRESSING

This is a splendid combination of textures, colors, and tastes.

2 pounds fresh green snap beans
1 15–16-ounce can chick-peas
1 15–16-ounce can red kidney beans

4 ounces filberts, coarsely chopped

CREAMY VINAIGRETTE DRESSING
1 egg yolk
3 tablespoons tarragon vinegar
½ teaspoon Dijon or similar mustard
½ cup peanut or vegetable oil

¼ cup fruity olive oil, or ¼ cup additional peanut or vegetable oil
Salt and pepper to taste
2 tablespoons finely minced green onion (optional)

To prepare Creamy Vinaigrette Dressing: In a medium bowl, beat egg yolk with vinegar and mustard until creamy smooth. Add the ½ cup of oil, a few drops at a time, beating as added. When dressing begins to thicken, beat in remaining oil in a slow, steady stream. Season with salt and pepper to taste. If desired, stir in green onion. Cover and refrigerate until ready to use.

Cook green beans in a large pot of rapidly boiling water until crisp-tender. Drain into colander, then rinse briefly under cold running water to stop the cooking process. Blot dry and place in a large bowl. Add garbanzo beans, kidney beans, and filberts. Add Creamy Vinaigrette Dressing and toss to mix. Cover and refrigerate until ready to serve. If desired, serve with miniature muffins.
Makes 4–6 servings.

THREE-BEAN SALAD WITH CREAMY RADISH DRESSING

This is still one of the easiest and best salads ever.

1 small bunch radishes, trimmed, washed, and thoroughly dried

1 3-ounce package cream cheese, softened to room temperature

½ cup sour cream

1 tablespoon apple cider vinegar

2–3 dashes of Tabasco sauce (optional)

Salt and pepper to taste

1 15–16-ounce can red kidney beans, drained, rinsed, and blotted dry

1 15–16 ounce can black beans, drained, rinsed, and blotted dry

1 15–16-ounce can large lima beans, drained, rinsed, and blotted dry

1 cup trimmed and shredded romaine or iceberg lettuce (use inner leaves of 1 small head lettuce)

2 tablespoons chopped fresh basil leaves, or ½ teaspoon dried basil

6–8 large whole leaves romaine or iceberg lettuce, trimmed

Place radishes in the bowl of a food processor and process until finely chopped, or place on a chopping board and chop with a sharp knife. Set aside.

Place cream cheese in a large bowl. Add sour cream, vinegar, and, if desired, Tabasco sauce. Whisk until smooth. Season to taste with salt and pepper. Stir in radishes. Add beans, shredded lettuce, and basil. Toss thoroughly. If desired, cover and refrigerate until 30 minutes before serving. Spoon salad into lettuce-lined bowl.

Makes 6–8 servings.

WHITE BEAN SALAD WITH HAM

Here is a happy, hearty make-ahead salad to bring to a potluck supper. Though this salad can be put together in many different ways, we found this one to be the most flavorful.

*1 cup dried Great Northern or
similar white beans
8 ounces baked Virginia ham, cut
across into narrow strips and
strips cut in half
½ cup Italian Vinaigrette Dressing
(see page 135)
1 large Vidalia or other mild
onion, peeled and cut across
into very thin slices and broken
into rings*

*1 medium-size carrot, trimmed
and cut across at a 45-degree
angle into thin slices
½ cup minced parsley*

Place beans in a large pot and cover by about 2 inches with cold water. Let stand several hours or overnight. Drain beans and return to pot. Add water to cover by about 2 inches. Simmer over medium heat for about 1 hour. Add ham and continue to simmer until beans are tender. Drain into colander, then transfer to a large bowl. Add ¼ cup of Italian Vinaigrette Dressing and toss lightly to mix. Let stand at room temperature for about 1 hour.

Place remaining ¼ cup of dressing in a medium bowl. Add onion and carrot. Let stand at room temperature for about 1 hour. Add to bean mixture. Cover and refrigerate for 12–24 hours before serving. Transfer to salad bowl and sprinkle with minced parsley.

Makes 6 servings.

WHITE BEAN SALAD WITH WALNUT SAUCE

You can prepare this sauce a day ahead, but add the lettuce just before serving.

1 *large ripe tomato*
1 *medium-size cucumber*
 Salt
2 *tablespoons red wine vinegar*
3 *tablespoons water*
½ *cup coarsely chopped walnuts*
1 *small white onion, coarsely chopped*
1 *clove garlic, coarsely chopped*
¼ *tablespoon walnut, peanut, or vegetable oil*

Coarsely ground black pepper to taste
2 *tablespoons minced parsley*
3½ *cups cooked navy beans (see page 126, or 2 16-ounce cans small white beans, drained, rinsed, and blotted dry*
1 *cup shredded romaine or iceberg lettuce*

Cut tomato in half and squeeze out all seeds. Cut halves into narrow strips and spread out on paper toweling to drain. Peel cucumber, cut in half lengthwise, and scrape out seeds. Cut halves into small chunks. Place on paper toweling, sprinkle lightly with salt, and let stand 15–20 minutes. Rinse and blot dry.

Place vinegar, water, walnuts, onion, and garlic in the bowl of a food processor or blender. Add oil and process or blend to a coarse, chunky mixture. Scrape into a large bowl and season with 1 teaspoon of salt. Add pepper to taste. Stir in parsley, tomato, cucumber, and beans. If desired, cover and refrigerate 30 minutes before using. Add lettuce just before serving. Correct flavor with additional salt and pepper.

If desired, serve with Cauliflower with Anchovies (see page 156).

Makes 6–8 servings.

BEAN SALAD WITH PINEAPPLE SOUTHERN-STYLE

This classic southern salad made with old-fashioned boiled dressing has been updated with crisp, crunchy mung bean sprouts.

Creamy Pineapple Dressing (see below)

1 8-ounce can pineapple tidbits in heavy syrup, drained and syrup reserved

1 15–16-ounce can red kidney beans

1 10-ounce package frozen lima beans

1 cup (firmly packed) mung bean sprouts, rinsed and drained

1 small green pepper, chopped

½ cup thinly sliced celery

CREAMY PINEAPPLE DRESSING

Reserved liquid from canned pineapple

½ cup apple cider vinegar

1 tablespoon cornstarch

1 teaspoon dry mustard

2 teaspoons sugar

1 teaspoon salt

¼ cup peanut or corn oil

Coarsely ground black pepper to taste

1 tablespoon minced fresh dill weed

To prepare Creamy Pineapple Dressing: In a small saucepan, blend pineapple juice, vinegar, cornstarch, mustard, sugar, and salt. Cook and stir over medium heat until thickened (about 5 minutes). Remove from heat and gradually beat in oil. Stir in pepper and dill weed. Cover and refrigerate until ready to use.

Place pineapple tidbits in a large bowl. Drain kidney beans into colander and rinse under warm water until water runs clear. Add to pineapple.

Cook frozen lima beans following package directions. Drain and add to kidney bean-pineapple mixture. Add remaining ingredients. Add Creamy Pineapple Dressing and toss to mix thoroughly. If desired, cover and refrigerate until about 30 minutes before serving.

Makes 4–6 servings.

"GO WITHS" FOR GREAT SALAD MEALS

6.

A truly great salad deserves more than just salty crackers, no matter how crisp, even if it's no more than a thick slice of crusty bread or Brushette (lightly toasted Italian-style bread rubbed with a cut clove of garlic and drizzled with fragrant olive oil).

To prepare authentic Brushette, start with a really great Italian-style bread, which is dense, chewy and, of course, grained, and has a crust that is crunchy yet yields to the touch. Cut into ½-inch slices and place under high broiler heat only until lightly browned on both sides but still soft in the center. Rub, while hot, with a peeled, cut clove of garlic and brush with fruity olive oil, only enough to coat the surface.

To prepare only a few slices of Brushette, pour about ¼ cup of olive oil into a large, heavy skillet and place over low heat. Add 3-4 cloves of garlic, crushed, and cook them, stirring occasionally, until light golden. Remove and discard garlic. Add only as many slices of bread as will fit into the skillet in 1 layer. Turn them quickly in the oil to coat each side, then raise the heat to medium high and, pressing the bread down with the back of a spatula, cook until lightly browned. If you like, you can spread Brushette with Classic Pesto sauce (see page 185) or Parsley Pesto (see page 186), or make American-style with Smithfield ham spread or anchovy paste.

Brushette can be made ahead (without any additional toppings) and placed in a large brown paper bag until ready to serve. With a well-made pasta salad and a glass of light wine, it's a memorable meal.

Italian bread sticks are also a wonderful accompaniment to a salad meal. For a light luncheon party menu, serve a pasta salad, Sliced Tomatoes Italian-Style, and crisp, long bread sticks wrapped in a thin slice of prosciutto ham.

For more elaborate menus you can serve either a great salad or a variety of 2 or 3 different ones. To round out the menu you can add such extras as a wonderful assortment of finger sandwiches, a selection of different cheeses, or marinated vegetables such as Vegetables à la Grecque.

Here is a collection of great "go with" recipes that we have found to be immensely satisfying additions to any main-course salad meal.

VEGETABLES À LA GRECQUE

The idea of poaching tender young vegetables in a flavorful broth originated in Greece. However, this delicious dish is now considered part of classic French cuisine. The vegetables can be prepared ahead in any quantity, covered, and refrigerated until ready to serve, then used as a simple first course or part of a buffet supper, or they can be drained and added to almost any composed salad: pasta, rice, grain, bean, or potato. For an easy pasta salad, combine the vegetables with just-cooked pasta. Toss and serve with or without flavorful mayonnaise.

You can prepare just 1 vegetable or any number of different ones in the same poaching liquid. Since each will require a different amount of time to cook, however, each should be prepared separately.

POACHING LIQUID WITH HERBS

1 cup clear fat-free chicken broth or water

1 cup water

½ cup olive, peanut, or vegetable oil

⅓ cup white wine vinegar

⅓ cup dry white wine or vermouth

2 teaspoons salt

1–2 small cloves garlic, peeled and crushed

1 teaspoon dried herbs (thyme, tarragon, basil, or oregano), or 1 tablespoon chopped mixed fresh herbs

Any or all of the following vegetables:

Small bite-size broccoli flowerets

Broccoli stems, trimmed and cut into 1-inch "sticks" or thin rounds

Cauliflowerets

Tender young green snap beans

Carrots, trimmed, scraped, and cut at a 45-degree angle into thin slices

Whole tiny white onions, peeled

Small mushrooms, wiped clean and trimmed, or large white mushrooms, trimmed and quartered

Celery hearts (tiny, white core), halved or quartered

Green peppers, cut into strips

Thick slices of small summer (yellow) squash

Brussels sprouts, halved, or tiny whole brussels sprouts, trimmed

Combine poaching liquid ingredients and pour into a large saucepan. Cover, bring to a boil, then lower heat and let liquid simmer for about 30 minutes. If desired, refrigerate marinade until ready to use; reheat before using.

Bring marinade to a full boil and add the vegetables, 1 at a time; let simmer until just crisp-tender. As cooked, remove each vegetable with a slotted spoon and place in a large bowl or individual bowls. Spoon a little of the marinade over the vegetables. After each vegetable is cooked, add additional broth or water, if necessary, and bring to a boil again before adding the next vegetable. When vegetables are cooked, let them cool to room temperature, then cover and refrigerate until ready to use.

Each vegetable will cook in a different amount of time, depending on its texture and how it is cut; for instance, carrot slices may take 5–10 minutes, while onions will take 15–20 minutes or more; green snap beans will cook, depending on size, in 4–5 minutes, while zucchini slices will be ready in 10 minutes or less. Watch the vegetable as it cooks, testing often with the point of a small, sharp knife. Remove as soon as crisp-tender and transfer to a bowl. When prepared, each vegetable can be stored separately or together in the refrigerator, covered with some of the cooking liquid.

Makes 3 cups of poaching liquid for 4–6 cups of vegetables.

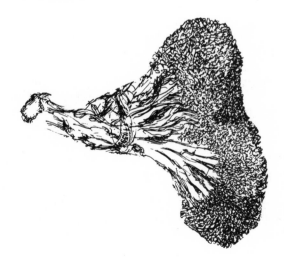

PICKLED VEGETABLES ITALIAN-STYLE

Use these vegetables as part of a large antipasto platter or add them to cooked pasta or rice for a great-tasting salad.

POACHING LIQUID

1½ cups white wine vinegar
½ cup mild virgin olive oil
1 tablespoon sugar, or to taste
1 tablespoon salt, or to taste

1 teaspoon dried oregano
Freshly ground black pepper
to taste

12–18 tiny white onions, peeled
1 cup cauliflowerets
2–3 carrots, trimmed, scraped, and cut into thin rounds
3–4 stalks celery, cut at a 45-degree angle into thick slices

1 small green pepper, seeded and cut into strips
1 small red chili pepper, trimmed and cut across into thin rounds
½ cup pitted black olives

In a saucepan, combine the poaching liquid ingredients and bring to a full boil. Add all of the vegetables and the olives. Lower heat, cover, and let cook for 3–4 minutes. Transfer vegetables and poaching liquid to a large bowl. Cover and refrigerate for at least 4 hours, preferably overnight. Vegetables can remain in the refrigerator 2–3 days. Drain before serving.

Makes 6–8 servings.

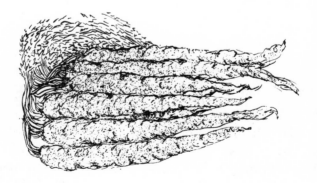

CAPONATA SICILIAN-STYLE

Here is a wonderfully flavorful addition to any salad buffet.

2 medium-size eggplants
½ cup olive oil
1 cup chopped celery
½ cup chopped onion
1 large tomato, peeled, seeded,
   and diced
3 tablespoons red wine vinegar

1 tablespoon sugar
¼ cup capers
   Coarsely ground black pepper
   to taste
   Salt (optional)
1 7-ounce can tuna, drained and
   flaked

Peel eggplant and cut into ½-inch cubes. Pour oil into a large, heavy skillet over medium heat. When hot add eggplant and cook, stirring frequently, until softened. Remove cubes with a slotted spoon and transfer into colander to drain. Add celery and onion to skillet. Lower heat and cook, stirring, until vegetables have softened. Add tomato. Cover and steam for about 1 minute. Uncover and cook, stirring, for about 5 minutes. Stir in vinegar and sugar. When sugar has dissolved, add capers. Season to taste with pepper. Add salt if desired, but keep in mind that capers are salty. Remove skillet from heat. Add tuna and stir to combine with other ingredients. Transfer mixture to a serving bowl. Cover and refrigerate until about 30 minutes before serving. Serve at room temperature.

Makes 8–10 servings as an accompaniment to a salad meal.

CAULIFLOWER WITH ANCHOVIES

This has a distinctive blend of flavors.

2 cups bite-size cauliflowerets
2 tablespoons mild olive oil
1-2 tablespoons white wine vinegar

1 small, flat can caper-stuffed
   anchovies, drained
1 tablespoon minced parsley
   Freshly ground black pepper

Fill a large, heavy skillet with water to a depth of about 2 inches; bring to a boil over high heat. Add cauliflowerets, cover and let steam for about 2 minutes. Uncover and cook, stirring, until crisp-tender. Drain into colander and rinse immediately under cold running water to stop cooking process. Transfer to a large serving bowl. Add remaining ingredients and toss. If desired, cover and refrigerate until about 30 minutes before serving. Serve at room temperature.

Makes 6–8 servings as an accompaniment to other salads.

CUCUMBERS IN SOUR CREAM

2 large cucumbers, sliced
1 cup sour cream
½ teaspoon salt
¼ teaspoon marjoram
1 tablespoon sweet basil wine
    vinegar, or 1 tablespoon plain
    vinegar and ½ teaspoon
    crushed basil leaves

2–3 tablespoons chopped chives
1 teaspoon dill seed
Freshly ground black pepper
    to taste

Place cucumbers in a medium bowl. In a small bowl, mix remaining ingredients. Pour over cucumbers and lightly mix. Cover and refrigerate for at least 1 hour before serving.

Makes 10–12 side servings.

MARINATED CUCUMBERS

Marinating cucumbers gives them extra-special flavor.

3 small to medium cucumbers,
  peeled and cut into thin slices
1 tablespoon salt
4 tablespoons white wine vinegar
½ teaspoon sugar

Generous sprinkling of imported
  Hungarian hot paprika
Coarsely ground black pepper
  to taste
¼ cup minced scallions

Place cucumbers in a medium bowl and sprinkle evenly with salt. Toss lightly to mix. Let stand at room temperature for about 1 hour. Pour off accumulated liquid and blot cucumbers dry with paper toweling. Transfer to a second bowl.

In a small bowl, combine vinegar, sugar, and paprika. Season lightly with pepper. Pour mixture over cucumbers. Add scallions. Cover bowl and refrigerate for 2–3 hours or overnight. Drain just before serving. **Makes 6–8 servings as an accompaniment to salad.**

PICKLED SHRIMP

This recipe comes from my file of old Charleston classics.

4 cups water
1 cup white wine vinegar
½ cup peanut or vegetable oil
1 large onion, chopped
1 large clove garlic, crushed

1 tablespoon mixed pickling
  spices
1 teaspoon salt
3 pounds medium or large shrimp,
  shelled and deveined

Pour water into a large saucepan; add vinegar, oil, onion, and garlic. Add pickling spices and salt. Bring to a full boil over high heat, then lower heat so that water simmers. Add shrimp and cook until firm and pink, 4–5 minutes. Remove from heat and cool slightly. Remove and discard garlic clove. Transfer without draining to a large storage bowl, refrigerate for 12–24 hours, then drain.

Add shrimp to pasta or rice salad, or serve on food picks with pre-dinner drinks.

If desired, mix 1–2 tablespoons of the pickling liquid with mayonnaise or sour cream to serve as a dip.

Makes 6–8 servings.

BLOODY MARY CARROTS

This recipe is not new. You may have it listed under "copper penny" carrots. Our version, made with nonalcoholic Bloody Mary mix instead of tomato soup, has more zip and zing, and we think you'll find it even better than the original.

2 pounds carrots, scraped and
    cut into ¼-inch rounds
1 medium-size Vidalia onion,
    peeled and chopped
1 cup nonalcoholic Bloody Mary
    mix

2 tablespoons spicy catsup
¼ cup peanut or vegetable oil
¾ cup sugar
¾ cup apple cider vinegar
2–3 dashes of Tabasco sauce
    Salt to taste

In a large pan of rapidly boiling water, cook carrots until crisp-tender. Drain into colander. Blot thoroughly dry, then transfer to a large bowl. Stir in onion.

In a medium bowl, combine remaining ingredients and stir to mix thoroughly. Pour over carrot-onion mixture. Cover bowl and seal with plastic wrap. Refrigerate for 12–24 hours before serving. Drain just before serving and transfer to a decorative serving bowl.

Makes 8–10 servings as an accompaniment to a main-course salad.

Sliced Tomatoes Sicilian-Style

A delicious way to serve sliced tomatoes.

4 large sun-ripened tomatoes
1 small red onion
1 cup Sicilian cracked green
  olives in brine, drained and
  coarsely chopped

¼ cup thinly sliced celery
Mild virgin olive oil
Red wine vinegar
Salt and pepper to taste

Cut tomatoes across into thick slices. Peel and thinly slice onion. Arrange tomatoes and onions in alternate rows on a large oval or round platter. Sprinkle with olives and celery. At the table, drizzle with oil and vinegar. Season lightly with salt and pepper.

Makes 6–8 servings as an accompaniment to a main-course salad.

Tunisian Eggplant

Eggplant should be used more often in this delicious way.

1 medium-size eggplant (about 1
  pound)
1 large red or green bell pepper,
  seeded and chopped
½ cup olive oil
⅓ cup red wine vinegar
1 teaspoon crumbled oregano

1 teaspoon salt
1 large tomato, seeded and
  chopped
½ cup chopped pitted black olives
1 7½-ounce can chunk-style tuna,
  drained and flaked
4 ounces feta cheese, crumbled

Peel eggplant and cut into 1-inch cubes. Place on steamer rack in steamer pot over simmering water until cubes are tender, 3–5 minutes. Transfer to a large bowl and add red or green pepper. In a small bowl, combine oil, vinegar, oregano, and salt. Beat with a fork until blended. Pour over eggplant-pepper mixture. Cover and refrigerate for about 1 hour.

Drain marinade from eggplant and set aside. In a serving bowl, place eggplant mixture, tomato, olives, tuna, and about 1 tablespoon of marinade. (Reserve leftover marinade for other use.) Toss to mix. Sprinkle with cheese.

Makes 6–8 servings.

MARINATED MUSHROOMS

These tasty mushrooms are a great addition to any relish tray, as are the Pickled Onions and Peppers.

12 ounces medium or large fresh mushrooms
¼ cup fruity virgin olive oil
1 tablespoon white wine vinegar
1 clove garlic, crushed

1 teaspoon salt
¼ teaspoon coarsely ground black pepper
2 tablespoons minced chives for garnish

Wash and trim mushrooms. Blot thoroughly dry. In a medium bowl, combine oil, vinegar, garlic, salt, and pepper. Add mushrooms. Cover and refrigerate overnight. Drain. Remove and discard garlic. Place in a decorative serving bowl and sprinkle with chives.

Pickled Onions and Peppers

8 ounces pearl onions
1 green bell pepper, seeded and
  cut into narrow strips
1 red bell pepper, seeded and cut
  into narrow strips

1 8-ounce jar gherkin pickles
Coarsely ground black pepper

Peel and cook onions as directed on pp. 153–54. Drain and place in a medium storage bowl. Add pepper strips and liquid from pickles. Cut pickles into thin slices and add to mixture. Toss to mix. Cover and refrigerate for 2–3 days or until ready to serve. Drain just before serving and transfer to a decorative bowl. Sprinkle with pepper to taste.

Piquant Cucumbers

3-4 medium-size cucumbers
½ cup sour cream

1 tablespoon Dijon mustard

Peel cucumbers, cut in half, and scrape out center seeds. Cut halves across into ¼-inch slices.

In a small bowl, combine sour cream and mustard. Stir in cucumber slices. Refrigerate until ready to serve.

Makes 4 servings.

TOMATOES WITH CAPERS AND PARSLEY

2 large sun-ripened tomatoes
1 tablespoon good quality olive
  oil
1 teaspoon red wine vinegar

¼ cup finely minced parsley
1 tablespoon capers
Coarsely ground black pepper

Cut tomatoes into thick slices and arrange on oval or round platter, slightly overlapping. Combine oil and vinegar and sprinkle evenly over slices. Sprinkle with parsley, capers, and pepper. Let stand at room temperature until ready to serve.

Makes 4 servings.

SANDWICHES TO COMPLETE A MAIN-COURSE SALAD

WATERCRESS SANDWICHES WITH WALNUTS
½ cup minced watercress
½ cup finely chopped walnuts
3–4 ounces imported French Petit
  Suisse (double crème cheese),
  or 1 3-ounce package American cream cheese, softened to
  room temperature and mixed
  with 1 tablespoon heavy
  cream
12 thin slices white or whole
  wheat bread, crusts removed

Combine watercress, walnuts, and cheese in a bowl. Beat with a fork until well blended and smooth.

Spread 6 slices of bread with the filling. Cover with remaining bread slices and cut in half.

Makes 12 sandwiches.

SHALLOT BUTTER SANDWICHES
The small effort it takes to prepare the filling for these sandwiches is well worth it.

4 ounces (1 stick) unsalted butter,
  softened
1 tablespoon minced fresh parsley
1 tablespoon minced shallots
¼ cup dry white wine
½ cup chicken broth, canned or
  homemade

Salt to taste
1 teaspoon coarsely ground black
  pepper
16 very thin slices white or whole
  wheat bread, crusts removed

In a small bowl, mix butter with parsley.

In a small saucepan, combine shallots, wine, chicken broth, salt, and pepper. Place over medium heat and let simmer until reduced to about 1 tablespoon of liquid. Remove from heat and cool to room temperature. Add to butter mixture and beat with a fork until blended.

Spread 8 slices of bread with the butter mixture and top each with a second slice. Cut sandwiches across into 2 finger strips. If desired, wrap in lightly moistened paper toweling. Refrigerate until ready to serve.

Makes 16 sandwiches.

PARSLEY BUTTER FINGERS

The trick to making these sandwiches taste very special is to mince—not chop—the parsley so finely that when you pick it up in your hand it holds together without falling apart.

6 ounces (1½ sticks) butter, softened

1 tablespoon anchovy paste (or about 4 anchovy filets, drained and mashed to a paste)

1 teaspoon onion juice (see below)

¼ cup very finely minced parsley

24 very thin slices white or whole wheat bread, crusts removed

In a small bowl, combine butter, anchovy, and onion juice. (To obtain fresh onion juice, peel and cut a large Vidalia or purple onion in half. Hold a half over a small bowl and with a small sharp knife scrape the cut half to obtain juice.) Beat with a fork until blended and fluffy. Stir in minced parsley.

Spread 12 slices of bread with the parsley butter mixture. Top with remaining slices. Press sandwiches together lightly. Cut lengthwise into 2 strips.

Makes 24 sandwiches.

BLACK OLIVE AND WALNUT TRIANGLES

½ cup minced black olives

½ cup chopped pecans or walnuts

2 3-ounce packages cream cheese, softened

2 ounces (½ stick) butter, softened

12 thin slices white or whole wheat bread, crusts removed

In a medium bowl, combine olives, walnuts, and cream cheese. Set aside.

Spread 6 slices of bread with butter. Spread 6 slices with olive mixture. Press slices together lightly. Cut each sandwich in half diagonally to make triangles.
Makes 12 triangle sandwiches.

PEANUT BUTTER AND CARROT SANDWICHES

½ cup peanut butter

2 medium carrots, shredded
  (about ⅔ cup)

¼ cup minced celery

¼ cup plain yogurt

¼ cup honey

4 large center slices sourdough or
  rye bread, crusts removed

In a medium bowl, mix together peanut butter, carrots, celery, yogurt, and honey until thoroughly blended.

Spread half of mixture on 2 slices of bread. Cover with remaining bread. Cut each sandwich into 4 triangles. If desired, cut edges of triangles. Save approximately 2 tablespoons of shredded carrots and use for dipping.
Makes 8 small triangle sandwiches.

MUFFULETTA

A Muffuletta is an Italian inspiration. A large, crusty round loaf of bread is cut across, then hollowed out and filled with any number of different salad mixtures. When ready to serve it is cut into pie-shaped wedges. *Mama mia!*

1 6½–7½-ounce can imported Italian tuna packed in olive oil

¾ cup finely chopped pitted alfonso or kalamata olives

¼ cup minced pitted Sicilian green olives

¼ cup chopped capers, well drained

½ teaspoon dried oregano

1 tablespoon minced fresh basil, or ½ teaspoon dried basil

6 tablespoons fruity Italian olive oil

3 tablespoons red wine vinegar

¼ teaspoon coarsely ground black pepper

1 1-pound round loaf Italian-style bread

1 cup shredded romaine or iceberg lettuce
4 ounces thinly sliced Genoa salami

4 ounces thinly sliced mozzarella
cheese

Several hours or a day ahead: In a large bowl, combine tuna, black and green olives, and capers. Season with oregano and basil. Stir in 6 tablespoons of olive oil and 3 tablespoons of vinegar, then sprinkle with pepper. Stir to mix. Cover mixture and refrigerate.

Cut bread horizontally and scoop out soft center. (Reserve center crumbs for other use.) In a small bowl, combine remaining 2 teaspoons of oil and vinegar and use to brush generously the bottom and top insides of the loaf. Add lettuce to olive mixture and toss to mix. Fill bottom of loaf with half of mixture. Cover with half of salami and half of cheese. Cover with remaining olive mixture, mounding it high, then pressing down lightly. Top with remaining salami and cheese, and then with remaining half of bread. Wrap and seal entire loaf in foil. Place on a large round plate and top with a second heavy plate; weight the plate down with 2 large unopened cans. Place in refrigerator for about 2 hours or until ready to serve.

To serve: Unwrap and place loaf on a large round platter. Cut into pie-shaped wedges but leave loaf intact.

Makes 8 large wedges.

Tomato Sandwich Rounds

4 ounces (1 stick) sweet butter,
softened to room temperature
1–2 dashes of Tabasco sauce
1–2 teaspoons freshly squeezed
lemon juice
24 thin slices white or whole
wheat bread

3 firm ripe tomatoes
1 small bunch watercress, with
stems removed and large
leaves torn into small pieces

Place butter in a small bowl. Stir in Tabasco sauce and lemon juice.

Using a large cookie or biscuit cutter, cut each bread slice into a round. (Reserve leftover bread trimmings for other use.)

Spread each bread round very lightly with butter mixture. Place rounds in a single layer on a large baking sheet (or sheets) and place in refrigerator until butter is firm, 20–30 minutes.

Cut rounded top from each tomato, then cut vertically (from top to bottom) into ¼-inch slices. (Reserve tops and end pieces for other use.)

Cover half of bread rounds with a tomato slice, sprinkle with watercress leaves, and top with second bread round. Press sandwiches together lightly, then cut across into 2 halves. If desired, stack sandwiches and wrap in lightly dampened clean dish towel, or double wrap in paper toweling and sprinkle lightly with water. Refrigerate until ready to serve.

Makes 24 sandwiches.

Toasted Pita Bread
with Tahini

2 cloves garlic, peeled and
coarsely chopped
½ cup fresh lemon juice
Salt
1 cup tahini (sesame seed)
paste

¼–½ cup cold water, if needed
½ cup finely minced parsley
6 pita bread rounds

Place garlic, lemon juice, and ½ teaspoon of salt in the bowl of a food processor or blender. Process or blend until smooth. Pour into medium bowl. Add tahini and stir with a fork to a smooth paste, adding water as needed. Stir in parsley and additional salt to taste.

Preheat oven to 350 degrees Fahrenheit.

Split pita bread rounds in half horizontally. Spread each half with tahini mixture. Cut each into 4 wedges. Place in oven until crisp, about 15 minutes. Serve warm or at room temperature.

If desired, place wedges loosely in a plastic freezer bag. Seal bag and store in freezer until ready to use.

Makes 48 wedges.

GARLICKY PITA BREAD TRIANGLES

2 large pita bread rounds
3 tablespoons mild, fruity olive oil
6 cloves garlic, peeled and crushed

1 teaspoon dried basil
3 tablespoons butter
Sprinkling of salt

Preheat oven to 350 degrees Fahrenheit.

Split pita rounds in half horizontally. Cut each half into 4 wedges.

Pour oil into a small, heavy skillet over very low heat. Add garlic and basil. Cook, stirring frequently, until garlic is limp. Remove and discard garlic. Remove from heat. Add butter and stir until melted; season with salt. Brush mixture evenly over each pita triangle. Place on a baking sheet. Bake until crisp, about 5 minutes.

Makes 16 triangles.

ONION ROLLS

1 tablespoon peanut or vegetable
  oil
1 small Vidalia onion, chopped
3 tablespoons butter, softened to
  room temperature

¼ cup minced parsley
4 large crusty French rolls

Preheat oven to 400 degrees Fahrenheit.

Pour oil into a small, heavy skillet over very low heat. Add onion and cook, stirring, until light golden in color and very limp, about 10 minutes. Remove skillet from heat and stir in butter and parsley.

Cut rolls in half horizontally and spread cut side with butter mixture. Place on a baking sheet. Bake until hot, about 5 minutes. Serve warm.

Makes 4 servings.

CREOLE-STYLE HOT AND SPICY CHEESE ROUNDS

4 large round French or Italian
  rolls
1 tablespoon Pommery or Creole-
  style mustard

2 tablespoons bottled spicy catsup
4 ounces mild cheddar cheese,
  chopped

Preheat broiler oven.

Split rolls in half horizontally.

In a small bowl, combine mustard, catsup, and cheese.

Mound mixture generously on each roll half and press down lightly. Place on a baking sheet about 3 inches under broiler heat. Broil until cheese is melted and bubbly hot.

Makes 4 servings.

CHICKEN, SHRIMP, OR TUNA SANDWICHES

1–1½ cups minced cooked chicken or canned tuna, or 1½ pounds cooked shrimp, peeled, deveined, and minced
½ cup minced celery
1 small Vidalia or purple onion, peeled and minced
½ small green pepper, seeded and minced
2 tablespoons finely minced mixed sweet pickles or small capers, drained
2 tablespoons minced parsley
1 hard-cooked egg white, finely minced
1 hard-cooked egg yolk
About ½ cup thick mayonnaise (or sufficient to hold mixture together)
1–2 teaspoons white wine vinegar or fresh lemon juice
Salt and pepper to taste
4 tablespoons (½ stick) butter, softened
12 thin slices white or whole wheat bread

In a large bowl, combine chicken, celery, onion, green pepper, pickles, and parsley. Stir in hard-cooked egg white.

In a small bowl, mash egg yolk until smooth. Stir in mayonnaise and white wine to make a thick mixture. Season to taste with salt and pepper. Add to salad mixture and stir with a fork to blend thoroughly.

Spread butter on 1 side of each slice of bread. Spread 6 slices with the filling. Top with remaining slices. Cut each sandwich in half to make finger strips or triangles.

Makes 12 finger strips or triangles.

SPECIAL SALAD DRESSINGS

7.

CLASSIC VINAIGRETTE DRESSING

To give you exact quantities of each ingredient for this classic mixture is as ridiculous as giving you exact measurements for salt and pepper in any recipe; it's simply a matter of taste. The usual proportions are 3 parts of oil to 1 part of vinegar, ½ teaspoon of salt, and a sprinkling of pepper.

6 tablespoons fruity olive oil
2 tablespoons red or white wine
   vinegar

½ teaspoon salt
Sprinkling of pepper

In a small bowl, combine oil and vinegar and whisk until well blended. Stir in salt and a generous sprinkling of pepper. Taste and adjust seasoning to your liking, adding a little of each ingredient until you're satisfied with the results.

Makes ½ cup of dressing, sufficient for a pasta, rice, bean, or potato salad to serve 4–6 people.

NOT-SO-CLASSIC VINAIGRETTE DRESSING

This is our own version of a basic, all-purpose vinaigrette dressing. You can, of course, vary the quantity of each ingredient to suit your own taste. Sugar is optional. If using a very fresh and, therefore, sweet-tasting olive oil, sugar isn't needed, but we have found it adds an extra dimension of flavor without making the dressing in the least bit sweet.

1 teaspoon salt
½ teaspoon sugar (optional)
¼ teaspoon coarsely ground black
   pepper
3 tablespoons vinegar: red or
   white wine, sherry, cider, or
   what have you

¾ cup mild virgin olive oil, or half
   olive oil and half peanut, vegetable, or corn oil

Place salt, sugar, and pepper in a bowl and add vinegar. Whisk until sugar has dissolved. Slowly add oil, beating as added. Continue to beat until mixture is smooth and creamy.

Makes about 1 cup.

VINAIGRETTE DRESSING SOUTHERN-STYLE

1 tablespoon Dijon or Creole-style mustard
¼ cup red wine vinegar
1 teaspoon sugar
½ teaspoon salt

½ teaspoon coarsely ground pepper
½ cup peanut or vegetable oil
¼ cup mild, fruity olive oil
1 tablespoon minced fresh chives

Place mustard in a small bowl. Add vinegar, sugar, salt, and pepper. Beat with a fork until well blended. Add peanut oil in a slow, steady stream, beating as added. Beat in olive oil and mix in chives. If desired, cover and refrigerate until about 30 minutes before using. Beat to re-blend before adding to salad.

Makes about 1 cup.

VINAIGRETTE DRESSING WITH HERBS

We especially like this dressing for pasta salads.

¾ cup mild virgin olive oil, or half
olive oil and half peanut, vegetable, or corn oil
2 cloves garlic, peeled and finely
minced
2 tablespoons chopped fresh
basil, or ½ teaspoon dried basil

1 teaspoon dried oregano
⅛ teaspoon dried rosemary
1 teaspoon salt
3 tablespoons red wine vinegar

Pour oil into a small, heavy skillet over low heat. Add garlic, basil, oregano, rosemary, and salt. Cook, stirring, until garlic is transparent and soft. Scrape mixture into a small bowl. Add vinegar and beat with a fork until well mixed.

Makes about 1 cup.

GARLICKY VINAIGRETTE DRESSING

The addition of fresh garlic to Classic Vinaigrette Dressing gives it a dramatically different flavor—hearty and earthy.

¾ cup mild virgin olive oil, or half
olive oil and half peanut, vegetable, or corn oil
3 cloves garlic, peeled and split in
half lengthwise

1 teaspoon salt
½ teaspoon coarsely or freshly
ground black pepper
3 tablespoons red wine vinegar

Place oil in a small, heavy skillet over low heat and add garlic. Cook, stirring, until garlic turns a light golden color. Remove and discard garlic. Pour oil into a bowl and add salt and pepper. Bring to room temperature. Add vinegar and beat until thoroughly blended. **Makes about 1 cup.**

Sweet and sour salad dressing

This is especially delicious with bean or rice salads.

⅓ cup sugar
1 teaspoon dry mustard
1 teaspoon salt

⅓ cup red wine vinegar
1 cup olive or salad oil

In the bowl of a food processor or a blender, combine sugar, mustard, salt, and vinegar. Add oil in a slow, steady stream until well blended. **Makes about 1⅓ cups.**

Mustard dressing

2 tablespoons basil vinegar
2 tablespoons fresh lemon juice
2 tablespoons Dijon or similar mustard
1 teaspoon sugar

¼ teaspoon salt
¼ teaspoon pepper
2–3 basil leaves, torn into small pieces (optional)
1 cup olive or salad oil

Place vinegar, lemon juice, mustard, sugar, salt, pepper, and basil in a medium bowl. Beat with fork until blended. Add oil in a slow, steady stream, beating until well blended. **Makes about 1¼ cups.**

LOUISIANA-STYLE VINAIGRETTE

¼ cup mild, fruity olive oil
½ cup peanut or vegetable oil
¼ cup red wine vinegar
1 teaspoon sugar

½ teaspoon salt
¼ teaspoon freshly ground black
  pepper, or to taste
Minced chives (optional)

In a small bowl, combine oils and vinegar and beat with a fork until blended. Beat in sugar, salt, and pepper. Add chives if desired.
Makes about 1 cup.

CREAMY RASPBERRY VINAIGRETTE

½ cup peanut or vegetable oil
¼ cup raspberry vinegar
1 tablespoon sour cream

½ teaspoon sugar
Salt and pepper to taste

In a small bowl, combine oil and vinegar. Beat with a fork until blended. Add sour cream and beat until smooth. Season to taste with sugar, salt, and pepper.
Makes about ¾ cup.

BLUE CHEESE VINAIGRETTE

½ cup light, fruity olive oil
1 tablespoon white wine vinegar
1 tablespoon fresh lemon juice
2 tablespoons crumbled blue
  cheese

2 tablespoons minced parsley
½ teaspoon grated lemon zest (yellow part of lemon rind)
Salt and pepper to taste

In a small bowl, combine oil, vinegar, and lemon juice. Beat with a fork until blended. Stir in cheese, parsley, and lemon zest. Season to taste with salt and pepper.

Makes about ¾ cup.

Peppery vinaigrette

½ small green bell pepper
½ small red bell pepper
½ cup virgin olive oil

2 tablespoons red wine vinegar
Salt and pepper to taste

Cut peppers from top to bottom into 4 wedges; remove all seeds and white ribs. Cut into small dice. Place in a small saucepan and cover by about 2 inches with water. Place over high heat and bring to a boil; let boil about 2 minutes. Drain into colander and blot thoroughly dry. Place in a small bowl. Add oil and vinegar. Stir to mix. Season to taste with salt and pepper.

Makes about ¾ cup.

Mustard shallot dressing

½ cup peanut or vegetable oil
3 tablespoons walnut oil
¼ cup red wine vinegar
½ small purple onion or 2 small
  shallots, chopped

2 tablespoons Creole or other
  grainy mustard
Salt and pepper to taste

Place all ingredients in an electric mixer. Mix on low speed until onion is minced and mixture is well blended. Season to taste with salt and pepper.

Makes about 1 cup.

Cumin dressing

3 tablespoons orange juice
1 tablespoon lemon juice
2 teaspoons ground cumin
1 teaspoon ground orange rind

1 teaspoon sugar
½ cup peanut or vegetable oil
Salt and pepper to taste

In a small bowl, combine ingredients and beat with a fork until well blended. Season to taste with salt and pepper.
Makes about ¾ cup.

Parmesan cheese dressing

½ cup peanut or vegetable oil
2 tablespoons apple cider vinegar
2 tablespoons freshly grated Parmesan cheese

½ small Vidalia or purple onion,
   or 2 small shallots, minced
Salt and pepper to taste

Place all ingredients in a large mason jar. Cover tightly with lid and shake to blend thoroughly. Or place all ingredients in a blender and blend until well mixed.
Makes about ¾ cup.

Green peppercorn dressing

¼ cup light, fruity olive oil
¼ cup peanut or vegetable oil
3 tablespoons raspberry or red wine vinegar

2 tablespoons green peppercorns
2 small shallots
½ teaspoon sugar
Salt and pepper to taste

Place all ingredients in the bowl of a food processor or blender. Process or blend until peppercorns and shallots are finely minced. Season to taste with salt and pepper.

Makes about ¾ cup.

HOMEMADE MAYONNAISE

HAND METHOD

1 whole egg
1 egg yolk
¼ cup white wine vinegar

½ teaspoon salt
¼ teaspoon white pepper
1¼ cups vegetable oil

In a small bowl, combine whole egg, egg yolk, vinegar, salt, and pepper. Whisk until smooth and about double in volume. Add oil in a slow, steady stream and continue to beat until very thick and smooth. Refrigerate until ready to use. Reblend just before using.

Makes about 2 cups.

PROCESSOR METHOD

2 egg yolks
¼ cup white wine vinegar
½ teaspoon salt

¼ teaspoon white pepper
1¼ cups vegetable oil

In the bowl of a food processor or blender, place egg yolks, vinegar, salt, and pepper. Process or blend until smooth and about double in volume. With motor running, add oil in a slow, steady stream and continue to blend until very thick. Refrigerate until ready to use. Reblend just before using.

Makes about 2 cups.

Sesame mayonnaise

1 whole egg
1 egg yolk
2 tablespoons soy sauce
2 tablespoons rice vinegar

1 tablespoon Oriental sesame oil
1 cup peanut or vegetable oil
Salt and pepper to taste

Place egg and egg yolk in the bowl of a food processor or blender. Process until blended. Add soy sauce and vinegar. Blend until smooth. With motor running, slowly add oils in a thin, steady stream, then continue to process or blend to a smooth, thick sauce. Transfer to a medium bowl and add salt and pepper to taste. (Remember soy sauce is salty.)

Makes about 1½ cups.

Mayonnaise niçoise

1 cup thick mayonnaise, prefera-
    bly homemade (see page 181)
1 tablespoon spicy catsup
1 tablespoon anchovy paste

1 tablespoon drained capers
1 tablespoon finely chopped
    Niçoise olives
¼ teaspoon oregano

In a small bowl, combine mayonnaise, catsup, and anchovy paste. Stir until smooth. Add capers, olives, and oregano and stir with a fork until well blended.

Makes about 1¼ cups.

GARLICKY MAYONNAISE

1 egg yolk	½ cup light, fruity olive oil
1 whole egg, at room temperature	¼ cup peanut or vegetable oil
2 tablespoons fresh lemon juice	Salt and pepper to taste
1 clove garlic, chopped	

Place egg yolk, whole egg, lemon juice, and garlic in a blender and blend until garlic is minced. With motor running, add olive oil in a thin, steady stream. Add peanut oil and continue to blend until mixture is smooth and thick, scraping down sides of jar if necessary. Season to taste with salt and pepper.

Makes about 1¼ cups.

CILANTRO MAYONNAISE

1 cup mayonnaise	2 tablespoons finely minced
2 tablespoons fresh lime juice	fresh cilantro*
2–3 dashes of Tabasco sauce	Salt and pepper to taste

In a medium bowl, combine mayonnaise, lime juice, and Tabasco sauce. Stir in cilantro. Beat with a fork until well blended. Season to taste with salt and pepper.

Makes about 1 cup.

*Cilantro: In Spanish-speaking markets, coriander is widely known as cilantro. It is also known as Chinese parsley.

CHAMPAGNE DRESSING

1 egg yolk
1 teaspoon Creole or other flavor-
    ful mustard
2 tablespoons champagne vinegar
½ cup safflower, peanut, or corn
    oil
    Salt and pepper to taste

In a small bowl, beat egg yolk with mustard and vinegar until smooth.
Add oil in a slow, steady stream, beating as added. Season to taste
with salt and pepper.
Makes about 1 cup.

MANGO CHUTNEY DRESSING

½ cup mild, fruity olive oil
2 tablespoons red wine vinegar
1 tablespoon sour cream
1 teaspoon Pommery mustard

2 tablespoons mango chutney
    (large pieces of mango cut into
    small slivers)
    Salt and pepper to taste

In a medium bowl, combine oil and vinegar. Whisk until well blended.
Beat in sour cream and mustard. Add chutney and stir to mix. Season
to taste with salt and pepper.
Makes about ¾ cup.

Horseradish dressing

3 tablespoons mayonnaise, preferably homemade (see page 181)
½ cup sour cream
1 tablespoon bottled horseradish

1 teaspoon Dijon or similar mustard
Salt and pepper to taste

In a small bowl, combine mayonnaise, sour cream, horseradish, and mustard. Beat with a fork until well blended. Season to taste with salt and pepper.
Makes about ¾ cup.

Classic pesto

This elegant classic has many versions as well as many uses. Prepare it when fresh basil can be had in abundance, then freeze it in small containers to have on hand for every month of the year.

¾ cup fresh basil leaves, washed
   and patted thoroughly dry
2 cloves garlic, peeled, crushed,
   and minced
¾ cup top-quality light, fruity
   olive oil

1 teaspoon sherry wine or white
   wine vinegar
½ cup grated Parmesan cheese
½ cup pine nuts
Salt and pepper to taste

Place basil, garlic, and oil in the bowl of a food processor or blender and process or blend until smooth. Add vinegar, cheese, and pine nuts and process very briefly. Season to taste with salt and pepper.
Makes about 1¼ cups, enough for 12–16 ounces of pasta.

OTHER WAYS TO USE CLASSIC PESTO
Stir about 1 tablespoon of Classic Pesto into store-bought or home-made mayonnaise.

Mix Classic Pesto with equal quantities of sour cream and use as a dressing for rice, bean, or potato salads.

Add about 1 tablespoon of Classic Pesto to a basic vinaigrette dressing and stir to mix.

Stir about 1 tablespoon of Classic Pesto into sandwich filling mixtures.

PARSLEY PESTO

This is a wonderfully lusty "pesto" for the winter months when large quantities of fresh basil are unavailable or too expensive to buy from your market.

1 large bunch (about 1 cup) fresh parsley
3 tablespoons crumbled dried basil leaves
1 clove garlic, peeled and coarsely chopped
¾ cup fruity olive oil

1 tablespoon red wine vinegar
Generous sprinkling of coarsely ground black pepper
⅓ cup pine nuts or walnuts
⅓ cup grated Parmesan cheese
Salt to taste

Remove tough stems from parsley and coarsely chop leaves. Place in the bowl of a food processor or blender. Add basil, garlic, about half of the oil, and the vinegar. Process or blend until ingredients are reduced to a chunky paste. With motor running slowly, add remaining oil. When oil has been incorporated, transfer mixture to a small bowl and stir in remaining ingredients. Add salt to taste. Use as a sauce for room-temperature pasta or as a spread for thick slices of Italian-style bread.

Makes about 1 cup.

UNCOOKED SUN-DRIED-TOMATO SAUCE FOR PASTA

Mix this lusty, strong-flavored sauce at room temperature into freshly cooked, drained, still-hot pasta. Serve at room temperature.

4–5 *canned sun-dried tomato*
  halves, drained
  2 *large firm ripe tomatoes,*
  peeled, seeded, and chopped
  ½ *cup pitted Niçoise olives*
  ½ *cup (tightly packed) fresh*
  basil leaves, or 2 tablespoons
  dried basil leaves, crumbled

⅓ *cup chopped walnuts*
⅓ *cup grated Parmesan cheese*
½ *cup light, fruity virgin olive oil*
  Salt and pepper to taste

Combine all ingredients in the bowl of a food processor or blender. Process or blend to a chunky sauce. Add salt and pepper to taste.
Makes about 1½ cups.

Index